Janea's Journey

Breaking the Chains of Domestic Violence

Written

By

Janea Page

Copyright © 2017 by Nspired Ascensions Inc.

All rights reserved. No part of this publication may be reproduced, distributed, or transmitted in any form or by any means, including photocopying, recording, or other electronic or mechanical methods, without the prior written permission of the publisher, except in the case of brief quotations embodied in critical reviews and certain other noncommercial uses permitted by copyright law. For permission requests, write to the publisher, addressed "Attention: Permissions Coordinator," at the address below.

Nspired Ascensions Inc.

www.nspiredascensionsinc.org

Table of Contents

Dedication i

Introduction iii

Chapter One 1
    Enjoying the Single Life 1

Chapter Two 4
    The Biggest Mistake 4

Chapter Three 12
    Falling for a Fool 12

Chapter Four 21
    Not His First Love 21

Chapter Five 28
    Nightmare on Heatherlea Dr. 28

Chapter Six 35
    Victim vs. Victim 35

Chapter Seven 43
    The Big Setback 43

Chapter Eight 51
    The Nightmare Continues 51

Chapter Nine 60
    Seeing it Through Until the End 60

Chapter Ten 69
    Finally, I Can Breathe 69

Chapter Eleven 78
    Moving ONE STEP FORWARD 78

Chapter Twelve 87
    Self Help Guide to Continuing Moving ONE STEP Forward ... 87

Resources 97

Acknowledgements	**100**
About the Author	**101**
A Grown Person	**103**

Dedication

This book is dedicated to women, men, and children who have suffered through domestic violence silently. May it Inspire and Empower you to use your VOICE and be a VOICE for others who continue to suffer with ABUSE in silence.

Introduction

None of us wants to be lonely or single. Outside of our family and friends, we have no one to share our thoughts and ideas with. We have no one to have a meaningful, intellectual, mind stimulating conversation with. Some of us "single people", as we are so naturally and respectfully called, have no life. Our lives consist of going to work, taking care of our children, going to church or finishing up our college degrees to make the time go by faster. But in the end, we are still lonely. Boredom sets in. Then we start to look at all the other couples around us and feel sorry for ourselves because they are "happy and booed up" and we are sitting back having a glass of whatever, wishing we were booed up. So, some of us began to go down the path of looking for love. Well, I just so happened to be one of those who ended up looking for love and found anything but love. In this book, you will see how following my own path led me down a road filled with destruction, lies, abuse and how I could come full circle to RRR, rebuild my faith, repair my heart and restore my soul.

Chapter One

Enjoying the Single Life

No one wants to be single. But after enduring two failed relationships from 2002 to 2009, single is exactly what I needed to be. After the second failed relationship in 2009, I began to realize I never gave myself time to heal between relationships and furthermore I wasn't ready for a new relationship with anyone. And another thing, most of the relationships I had been in were based on SEX. I was so damn tired of giving away pieces of my mind, body, and soul (mostly body) to men who did not care about anything else but sex because I never required them to. So yes, 2009 was the perfect time to begin the "the SINGLE LIFE" and besides, my children needed me more than anything or anyone.

Being single gave me time to reflect on the bad allowing me to begin to move forward and focus on the good and the three R's: REPAIR, REBUILD, RESTORE. Rebuild my faith because it was gone. Repair my heart because it was broken, and Restore my soul because it was lost and needed to be found. Singleness gave me time to clear my head renewing my thoughts and allowing more time and attention to be given to my children; but most importantly time to work on me. This also gave me time to stop accommodating and giving away pieces of me to people (mostly men) who were non-deserving. The single life has also put me in the mind frame of growing closer to God, healing my heart, finding my way, and finding love in due time. Until then, the single life it was.

There were some disadvantages to being single as well, but not many. Although I was enjoying my newly found singleness just like any single person I would get lonely. That is just a natural reaction. If I wanted to have a stimulating conversation all I had were my friends. I did not have a significant other to have this with. How would it look trying to have an adult conversation with my children who at that time were 3 and 11 years old? The most we would have talked about would probably be The Wonder Pets with my daughter and what new game should go with my game system for my son. Yeah, right. If I wanted to go out to the movies I would have to go with my friends and have dinner with them. I had no one I could laugh with on a consistent basis outside of my friends.

As I began to embark on this journey of new found singleness I found it hard to accept because I was not used to being alone. I had always had a man. Yeah, just a man, or maybe I should say the shell of man because hell, most of them acted like little boys who needed their mother more than wanting or needing the companionship of a woman or loving relationship. But every day, as I woke up as a single person I began to enjoy it. I enjoyed it tremendously. For once I was not bogged down or trapped in a non-meaningful relationship that was not headed anywhere. I was neither accommodating nor trying to please others. The only person I had to please was myself.

I enjoyed the fact that I could come and go as I pleased and if I chose to be bothered than I would. It was my choice totally left up to me. During this time, I also learned how to let people go as well. If the person had a negative vibe, demeaning or disrespectful disposition, I was not dealing with them and cut them off quicker than I met them. No if's, and's, or but's about it. The days of being disrespected were behind me and I was happy about it. I was starting to enjoy my life and the strides I had made since coming out of horrible relationships and who I was beginning to evolve into. Recognizing I'm a strong young black successful educated woman I could get to putting God first, my children's well-being and safety second, and family third. The only attachments I had were my children and making moves in my career and starting my own business. Yes, I was loving the new me at this point. That was all about to change.

After being in Nashville, TN for 15 years I made a career move that transitioned my family back to Indiana in 2010. Still single and loving life along with my children I tried to get adjusted to life in Indianapolis. But now I am little more cautious than what I was in Nashville because we were in a new city but nevertheless I am still enjoying myself. From February 2010 to June/July of 2011, things were cool. Dated but nothing serious. Men were still on the same old BS, not looking for a serious commitment and neither was I. Then, a chance email and phone call changed everything that I had worked so hard towards.

His name was Lee Moore. 6'2, very handsome and he has a muscular build, a barber by trade. We first met in 1997, at a club. I was 23 going on 24. We kept eyeing each other in the club. We exchanged numbers, and it went from there. The first go around, we dated for about 6-7 months and then broke up. We then got back in contact with each other for a second time right around the time my son turned 1. That did not go well because I was still angry and bitter over how our prior relationship ended. We tried again for the third time. My son was around 3 or 4. And that did not last long either.

You would have thought after several attempts of trying to make things that I would not consider trying to have another relationship with him. But no, I thought to myself "surely he has changed by now and everything should be just fine". So, I made the decision to talk to him. I thought it was harmless. He lived in Nashville, TN at the time and I was back here in Indiana. And it was a long distance, so I did not see any problems with us talking. And besides, I would be in control of the situation, or so I thought.

As I sit back and start to recollect everything, I wish I would have never opened the door that God had closed. He closed the door for a reason and closed it more than once, which meant he saw something that I did not see; a correction that I did not want to see. I was blindsided and unprepared as to what and who was on the other side of that door. God quickly showed me why I should have stayed single and continued to enjoy the single life.

Chapter Two

The Biggest Mistake

Around June or July of 2011, Lee had his teenage son at the time reach out to me. At first I did not respond because I had not seen his son in so long that I did not recognize who he was. I said to myself, "Who is this kid sending me a message and why"? A few weeks went by and I received another message from the same kid. This time the message was a little more personal stating who his father was and 2 phone numbers I could reach him at. When I recognized the name, I realized who had been trying to reach out to me. So, I decided what the hell, let me call and see what he is talking about.

A few days after I received the second message I called Lee. I remember the exact words I said to him. I said, "I heard you were looking for me", "What and why are you looking for me"? For a minute, you could hear a pin drop and then finally he said, "Yes, I have been looking for you". Later that day after our initial conversation we talked for a few hours on the phone more than once like we were teenagers still in high school. We reminisced over the short-lived relationship we had in the past and how his second marriage did not work out.

We talked about anything and everything. Then, during one of the conversations he uttered these words, "*You are the one. You have always been the one. It was me who was not ready. I want to be with you. I should have been with you way back then, but again, I was not ready*". And I thought to myself, "Really? I was the one". At first, I did not believe him, but as time went on, he started to prove to me more and more why I was the one or so I thought, but I will save that for later.

We started making plans to see one another. Our initial plans to meet each other were hampered as I was not able to travel due to my finances not being in order. So, he got on the Greyhound and came to see me for a few days in Indianapolis. It felt different being with someone after not being in a relationship for 2 years. I felt like, *"this is really happening. I am going to start all over with an old flame and we are going to make things work, again".* I remember when I drove down to the bus station to pick him up, he jumped into the car and immediately kissed me and back to my house we went. I'll say it again, MY HOUSE.

We stayed up and talked for hours. The next day, I was in my normal routine except this time I had an additional person there with me. I was thinking to myself, *"Are you sure you want to do this? Long distance relationships are hard. So, do you really want to do this"?* I wish I would have listened to my gut feelings. But I did not. While he was here, we drove around looking at different barber shops in the area because he was a barber by trade. Before you knew it, it was time for him to leave and go back to Nashville, TN. So back on the bus he went.

Then about a month later, me and my children went to visit him in Nashville, TN. It was a weekend trip. Got there and picked him up and off we went to the hotel room for 2 nights. This man could not wait to take my clothes off and get me in the bed and I did not stop him either. When it was all over, I was like, *"Really? You're kidding me, right'?* I was so ready to come back to Indy because after all, I did not have a good time but I tried to make the best of it. I got a phone call from Lee on Monday asking me what did I think about the visit, and I told him I thought it was okay. I wish I would had told the truth and stated my true feeling, but because I did not want to be alone, I told him I thought everything went well.

By the end of the week, he said he was ready to move up here because he did not want me here by myself. I asked him what was he going to do with his children, and he was like, *"For now, I*

am going leave them here with my parents until school is out here and then I will move them up here". I was against it because I do not believe a parent should leave their children with other people to raise and I voiced that opinion loudly thinking it would make him rethink his decision to move up here, but it did not. I did not voice it loudly enough because when it came down to it, I did not want to be alone. I never even thought about how this man moving in would affect my children. I just knew I did not want to be alone. About 3 weeks to a month after that conversation I was off to Nashville yet again. This time it was to pick him up and move him here so we could start a new life and new beginning. That was the worst decision I made.

He moved in 3 days before my daughter's 5th birthday. I had not told anyone in the family that he was here because of him not working, I did not want them to know he was here permanently living in my house with me and my children. Later on in the week, we had a birthday party for my daughter and my parents drove down from Gary, IN. I had talked to my mother about him, but I never told her he was moving in. So of course, it was a huge shock when he came down the steps and introduced himself to my parents and that he had officially moved here from Nashville, TN to live with us. My parents were like "WOW", but did not say anything to me at that moment because it was my daughter's birthday and that was more important at the time. Later on in the week, my mom called me and we had a conversation about Lee being there permanently. She asked me why I did not say anything to her or my dad about him moving down here and I remember saying to her, "I did not want to say anything because if it did not work, I did not want to get everyone all involved in this". She understood what I was saying, but I think her feelings were hurt because I never said anything and we would normally talk about things like this.

Things went on smoothly for a few weeks and then we had a big blow up the day of my cousin's birthday party and right before Thanksgiving in 2011. The blow up was all over a key. I don't remember what was said, but I do remember what happened. I was in the shower and he made a statement and I replied with a comment to his statement and before I knew it, he ran into the bathroom and snatched the shower door almost completely off the hinges. I was standing there like, "What the hell is wrong with you"? All I could see was rage in his eyes. He kept screaming at me and I was screaming and yelling back at him. Then, before I knew it, he took his hand and put it over my mouth, trying to keep me quiet, and stated, "Why are you yelling? Are you trying to make the neighbors think I did something to you"? I looked at him and once he removed his hand, I did not say anything. I kept begging to get out of the shower because he had me cornered and he would not let me out. I begged and pleaded with him to let me out so I could at least dry off and put some clothes on and all he kept saying was "No".

He finally let me out of the shower and once he did, I was trying to get my clothes on and get as far away from him as possible. He went from screaming to me in the shower to screaming to me in the bedroom. He was like, "Take me home. Take me back to Nashville, TN". I wish I would have taken him back right then on the spot, but instead, I said, "No, I am not taking you back. If you want to go back, you need to take a bus or find a way, but I am not taking you anywhere because I don't have to". By the time I had emerged from the room, my daughter was standing in her doorway, looking like, "Is my Mommy okay" and my son was at the bottom of the steps with a bat in his hands and he was ready to go to war.

As the day went on, I did not have anything to say to him and I questioned myself again, "Are you making the best decision for you and your children"? Why had I not just been truthful with myself and say no? But instead, I said to myself, "Well, he will never do this again and things will be okay". I was in the beginning process of denial because I had been by myself for so long or what seemed to be a long time for me and did not want to be alone anymore. So, I settled for this fraction of a damn man rather than just packing his ass up and shipping him back to the city and state he came from. I would soon learn why not taking him back to Nashville would be the biggest mistake I have ever made.

The old saying goes, "Opposites attract", accept he was nothing like me and his way of pursuing me was completely all talk because his actions were clearly and I do mean clearly, something totally different. You know the type. He looks good on the outside, tall and built caramel skin tone in complexion, and clean cut. But was all messed up on the inside. He talked about how when we dated back in the day (15 years ago), that I was the one. He talked about how his parents loved me and how I had always been the one and he should have never let me get away. He talked about how he had been raising his sons because their mother wanted nothing to do with them and how much of a family man he was. He also talked about how he was separated, not divorced, but separated from his wife, because she was on drugs and it did not want a family. He even talked about how he could make life better for us and the kids and that we together, would be a power couple. How could we a power couple? We weren't equally yoked.

Only part of the above was true. But again, because I did not want to be alone, I fell for the bullshit. Even knowing he was still married, I decided to be in a relationship with a legally married man, who although was legally separated, yet still legally married. I asked him why they were not divorced if he did not want to be with her and his answer went something like this: "We are not legally together and when the time comes for me and you to be married, I will file for a divorce then. Also, there is nothing wrong with starting a new relationship while ending an old one. I have no interest in her. All I want is you". That was another big mistake. Lee truly did not belong to me. He belonged to his wife, Kim, and the fact remained he was married and we could not have anything until he was completely divorced from her. But nope, I did not care, I kept going right along with the façade that everything was calm, cool, and collective. I think I was in love with the façade of a man wanting me and wanting to help take care of my kids, but the reality of it was he was in this for himself to see what he could gain.

A couple of months after the first incident had gone by and now January 2012. He got a phone call from his father regarding his oldest son and how he had been acting up and got jumped in a fight. Lee's father simply stated to him, "Son, your son can no longer live here with me and your mother. He must move to Indianapolis with you". His parents were not so much as elderly, but they were not in the shape to raise two teenage boys. Plans were made to send his eldest son to IN. Mistake number 2. I was not ready to be a mother to children whose mother wanted nothing to do with them. My children were still trying to get adjusted to this man being in our home and now this. There was not a conversation other than, "Dad, put him on the bus and we will pick him from the bus station". You see, Lee had it easy. Why move back to TN with nothing? He was not going to do that. That was too much like right.

So, not only did I have to get adjusted to this man that I should have let go, I now had to get adjusted to a kid that I knew nothing about other than he was deeply troubled. He came right after MLK day in 2012. We had to go through the process of getting him enrolled in school and all that good stuff that comes with it.

Another issue came about as my son, who was used to having his own everything, now had to share his room with someone he knew nothing about. My son had his own game system, cell phone, and computer. Well, Lee felt like my son should not have a phone primarily because his son did not have one and he would not step up and get him one. His son would take my son's phone and not let him use it. He would come into my room and take my computer and hide it under the bed. He would go to school and be the class clown. His father was being called to the school almost daily until one day the freshman principal placed his eldest son in an alternative school.

Now I had to get adjusted to being a parent to a kid who did not respect anyone, caused trouble, and a father who did not want to discipline; his way of disciplining him was not what I would call discipline but at any rate, I felt like this was better than anything. So again, I fell for the bullshit. I found myself disciplining his son more than him. Then one day, his son asked me for a hug. I gave him a hug and he squeezed me so hard that I had to tell him to let me go more than once. He kept hugging me tightly and I kept telling him to let me go. We fell to the ground and as I am trying to get up, he bit me. An overgrown teenager bite to the point that I had a bruise. I instantly got pissed and I tried to rip his son's head off his shoulders because I am an adult. "What the hell is a teenager doing biting me "? is what I was thinking. I went upstairs to inform his father of what had just happened and I be damned this dude (his father) goes in the bathroom and rolls a blunt as if what I said to him did not make a bit of damn difference or as if it did not matter to him what had just happened. It wasn't until after he smoked his blunt that he decided to say something and then take off his belt like he was going to whoop a teenage boy who was not affected by that at all. To him, it was a joke.

I recall not speaking with his son for almost a week. Lee then decides that he wants to have a conversation with me on why I am not speaking with his son. He told me that he was not going to have me treat his son disrespectfully, although, it was okay for his son to disrespect me. I remember stating this to him, "It doesn't state anywhere that I have to talk with him. He is a kid and you are his father and as his father, you should have taken control of the situation when I asked, but you did not, so therefore there is not any need for me to talk with him". But for some reason, I was the person in the wrong for what happened between me and his son and it was not his son's fault. At first, I was like, "is this what trying to blend a family is all about", but then I quickly started to realize, this is not how blending a family should work and this was beginning to be the biggest mistake ever in life. I sometimes wish I would had gotten out of this relationship beforehand, but not wanting to lose what I thought was a good thing, I stayed.

Chapter Three

Falling for a Fool

The more involved I began to get in this relationship, the more I realized I was falling for a complete fool. He was not measuring up to the man he claimed or portrayed himself to be. Lee seemed to be more clingy and needier than ever. He talked about how he was not a liar or how he did not have to lie to get his point across. He also wanted to look like the man, but he was not the man. He kept professing his love to me and I was falling for it, like a rock would fall off a cliff, hard and fast. It did not matter what anyone else had to say, I was in love with this man, who was now starting to show his true colors towards me, my family and my children.

There was an incident where we had a huge argument one morning and I was trying to get ready for work. I went to my closet to try to get clothes out to wear and when I tried one last time, he responded like this, "Keep pulling clothes out of the closet and I am going to throw all of the clothes in the closet out all over the place". I was like what the hell, so to keep the peace and save face, I stopped pulling clothes out of the closet. I went into the bathroom and started to cry as he had told me I needed to leave. Leave at home that had my name on it. I looked at him and said to myself out loud, "This is my house. Why should I have to leave my house"? The next thing I knew, he balled up his fist and with his other hand, he pulled my hair so tight my entire head was on fire. He then said, "What did you say about this house"? I retracted my statement and was like, "I did not say my house. I said our house". By the time I had made it out of the bathroom, suddenly he came out of his rage. I grabbed my daughter as my son was already at school and left the house in a panic.

Later that night, he wanted to talk. And we talked about the same old thing. Like how I should not have provoked him or I need to watch what I say and I thought to myself again, "I am a grown ass woman; why do I need to watch what I say"? He also kept saying that I don't know how to communicate and I should not yell all the time. My thought, "how do you expect for me to respond when you are pulling my hair, screaming at me, tossing me around like a rag doll and so on"? I just kept looking at him like, "Are you freaking serious? You must be out of your freaking mind"? But again, this the fool I was falling for and furthermore, I never let anyone know what was truly going on. I kept it hidden from everyone; only my kids and his kids knew.

As I began to sit and start to re-evaluate things, I became enraged with the events of the day and I began to tear up at my desk. The desk that I purchased with my own money. I picked up the bat and started to beat the desk because I needed something to take my frustration out on and I could not take it out on my kids or his for that matter. As the desk started to come apart, I was getting ready to throw pieces of it down the steps and both his son and my son came and were like, "we are not going to let you throw that down the steps. We are not going to let you break anything else because of him". I kept telling them to move because I was determined to get that desk down the steps. I was so full of hate, rage and anger against this man and what he was doing with my life, rather what I was allowing him to do with my life. Life should not be this hard for two people who claimed to love each other.

The more I started to be around him, the more I noticed I was beginning to pick up some of his ways. Instead of trying to communicate on an adult level, I would scream, yell and throw things. All signs of an abusive relationship or signs of Battered Women's Syndrome (BWS). I was in constant chaos and to me, it was all okay. I had no problem with it. I was in love with a damn fool. No if, ands, or buts about it. This was truly my life and it did not matter what the kids saw or what anyone had to say, I was staying in this for the long haul.

Then one day, Lee showed up to my job with roses and ring box and asked me to marry him. Of course, as a fool, I said yes. I remember taking a picture of my ring and calling my parents and letting them know that he proposed to me. My parents told us congrats and then my mother proceeded to say, "I am happy for you both, but if this is something that you all do not want to do, you can make the choice to walk away". Boy, I wished I would have listened back when she first said that. However, we continued with this façade that everything was okay, except for one thing, he was still married. Prior to him proposing to me, I would tell him that he needed to do the paperwork to be divorced from his present-day wife at the time. His comeback, "I dated Kim all the way up until we decided to get married. I went to Michelle (who Lee was still married to while dating Kim), and got the papers signed. His divorce went through and he and Kim got married. Well, that was the same process he wanted to do with me as well and again, he did not see an issue with him being married to someone else while being engaged to me.

I tried explaining to him, that each state is different and since he had been in IN for over a year, he would have to follow the regulations here. By this time, it is 2012. I pulled the paperwork for his divorce and even went so far as to fill it out for him and save it to my flash drive. What I did not notice at the time, is I was handicapping him from doing anything for himself. I was the one handling everything and I am not the one who was getting a divorce, it was him. He should have done all this prior to coming here, but in the famous words of Steve Harvey, "I never made this a requirement". I just went along with the bullshit.

Now comes the fun part. The entire divorce cost a whopping $160 and he wanted me to help pay for it. "Um, no, I do not think so. As much as you smoke, you can pay for this yourself. Take the weed money, save it, stack it. I do not care how you pay for it. I am not paying for it". And I did not. The reason being, me falling for this fool of a man, I was already paying for just about every bill in the house. Yes, he would make sure we would eat and from time-to-time, we would split the bills in half, but for the most part, it was all me. I flat out refused to pay for this. I had split my tax refund and refund from school with this man. I was not about to give another damn dime to him. So, needless to say, he never filed the papers. Life continued with us so called "being engaged" and Lee was still married to another woman, which he had no clue where she was, even if he wanted to start divorce proceedings.

By this time, it was spring 2012. His older son was still causing problems and it was only getting worse. His son clearly had a problem with respect and back talking. There was an incident at the pool at the apartment complex where we were living in at the time. The pool had just opened for the spring and summer and his older son went to the pool without a pool pass and proceeded to talk disrespectfully to the apartment complex manager. Well of course, this sent his father into a rage and here he goes down to speak with the complex manager. His father insisted on doing all the talking and like a dumb ass, I let him, because I am so in love with this fool. I informed the apartment manager that I was not resigning my lease and that this incident with his son would not happen again. She was okay with that and for once he made his son apologize. However, that was just one of many run-ins with the apartment complex manager and complex management. I was starting to notice, the reason why his son did not respect authority, is because his father did not respect it either. His motto was clear: "I do what I want, say what I want and when I want".

Before we moved out of the apartment, there was yet another incident. I can remember on this day, we had an argument that morning. Not sure what we were arguing about, but we had an argument. I can recall myself saying something to the effect of, "I hate my life and I just wish I would die". He was like, "Don't say that". I proceeded to walk out of the room and out of the house. He took my car keys, so I could not drive off. I could not take my daughter to daycare, so I just walked out of the door in tears. And of course, because he doesn't want anyone to know what is going on, we come running behind me calling my name and I am just crying, walking and screaming, "Lord, why me? What did I do that was so bad and undeserving to you to deserve this"?

He finally caught up with me and was pulling my arm back to the house and I kept pulling away from him. We finally made it in the house and I screamed at him how much I truly hated him and how he got on freaking nerves. I had a picture in my room. Lee was throwing things at me. So, in a fit of rage and anger again, I picked up a candle in a jar and dropped it on the picture. Glass went everywhere. I did not care. Then, as I tried to go to work, he would not let me go, he held me against my will and had me call my boss at a time to let her know I would not be there. My whole behavior was changing. I was stuck in the house with him, my daughter and his youngest son. Lost and in a fog, as to what had just happened, I was truly thinking, "Why am I with this man? He is a fool, but I am so in love with him, but why"? We went out to lunch with the kids and I can remember sitting there not even able to eat, crying my eyes out. I got up and went and sat in the car for the remainder of the time while they ate. Later that night, we talked and almost agreed to let each other go, which should have happened, but did not happen. Instead, we had sex and that was it, that was the make-up, but clearly I was seeing things differently.

There were several incidents after that, but one that was the most dramatic was right before we were set to move out of the apartment. Yet another argument with an unhappy person! I was getting ready for work and he was rambling about something and I was not paying him any attention. Instead of me taking my daughter to daycare, I left her there with his sons. A big mistake! He continued to call me and argue with me while I was on my way to work. By the time I had got to work, he was still talking crazy. He knew the one way to get me back to the house was to say something off the wall about my daughter. The last call he made to me he said, "You better come and get your daughter because I am going to leave her here by herself". I took an early lunch and clocked out to go and get her and take her to my uncle's house.

When I pulled up to the apartment, he came outside. I told him to just send my daughter out and we would leave, but instead, he was trying to get me to get out of the car. I refused. I kept driving forward and backing up. This went on for about 5-10 minutes. Then he stepped to where I almost ran over his foot (I wished I would have run him over instead, to be honest). I let the window down just a little bit too much and before I knew it, he had put his hand through the window enough to reach in and put the car in park. He then pulled me out of a locked, yes, a locked car, took my keys and dragged me into the house. This time though, the maintenance man was outside along with a group of women and they all witnessed what had taken place. He threw me into the house and slammed the door. From there he threw me up against the wall and threw off his watch to the ground. He then took my phone and threw it against the wall and it broke into pieces. As he had me cornered, I said to him, "So now what, are you going to hit me"? And he said, "No, I am not going to hit you, but just watch what I do to you", as he proceeded to toss me around like a rag doll and then there was a knock at the door. And the voice on the other side of the door said, "Open the door, it is the police". Yes, my chance to escape.

    As the police continue to knock on the door telling us to open it, Lee begins to beg and plead with me to let them know that everything is okay and that he will not do this again. I opened the door and the police proceed to ask me am I okay. I told him that I was okay and I just wanted to leave. The officers separated both of us and I went to my car and the other officer stayed in the house with him. The officer asked me was I being held against my will and I told him no. He continued to ask me the same question again, and I told him I just wanted to leave but I needed to get my daughter who was standing in the doorway looking to see if I was going to leave her. He allowed me to grab my daughter and I flew out of the driveway and back to work in total and utter shock as to what had just happened. I made it back to work, shaken and scared.

    I put my daughter in my office and proceeded to let my co-workers know what transpired. At that point, is when I felt like enough was enough. Myself, along with some of my coworkers, went back to the office complex and I had the manager, along with security, come and remove Lee and his sons out of my place. He was not allowed back on the premises. The security officers removed not only his sons, but him as well and that infuriated him. He was trying to get anyone and everyone to bring him up to my job. And then the phone calls began. First, I was a bitch this and bitch that. He went to my uncle's house asking my uncle whether his children could stay over there, but my uncle told him no. Then he continued to call me. By the time I had gotten off work, I had gone home and retrieved clothing for myself and my daughter as my son was out of town with a family friend.

We stayed at my uncle's house until that Friday and that is when we traveled back to Gary and I stayed with my parents to gain some type of clarity. I blocked his number so he could not call, all he could do was text, talking the same old bullshit. I still would not talk to him. At this point, I hated him all over again. I wanted nothing to do with him. I got rid of everything that belonged to him and his children and gave it to his friends. I did not care if they did not have a place to stay as I had enough of all the mess. I left my children in Gary for the week and when I got back to Indianapolis, he was calling, crying and begging, "I am sorry". I agreed to meet with him in a public place, and he tried to hold my hand and I snatched it back. I am sorry is all I heard and I did not care. I would not stay in my apartment, so I stayed with my cousin.

The next day he called. I met him at the gas station and he still was begging and trying to talk to me. Trying to give me money and then he was like, "No I need it for my kids". I told him I did not have time for his bs and the first thing that flew out of his mouth was, "FUCK YOU". And it caught him off guard when I told him that back. He said it again and I told him the same thing and then put his ass out of my car and went back to my cousin's house. I thought I was done, but then things took a turn that I did not even see coming.

I found a new place, but could not move in until August 10, 2012. Until then my children and I commuted daily from Pike Township to Warren Township. I still was not taking any of his phone calls and what was even worse, it was the first week of school and my daughter's first year of school. I would have to come to my apartment in the mornings to get her ready for school and myself ready for work. And who comes knocking on the door, this nut. To keep people from seeing him, I opened the door and did not talk to him.

Then one night, me and my cousin got into a heated argument right before we were ready to move into our new house. I was suddenly left with nowhere to go. The one person I did not want to call was the person I had to call because he had a place and we did not. I knew he did not want us out on the street or without anywhere to go. So, we stayed and then the second night we were there, a bad storm moved through and a tree fell on my car. I was like, "What the hell", because I did not want him moving with us, but then when he had to get his money back from his place due to the tree falling on my car and because I did not have car insurance at the time, I felt guilty and obligated to have him and his children move back in with us. And here we go with all the damn begging again.

Chapter Four

Not His First Love

So, as we settle into this 4 bedroom, 1200 square foot house, it was now clear that he was not going anywhere. This is not what I wanted because there had not been enough time for either of us to be together and he was still in this crying, begging and whining stage. He was starting to get on my nerves. But then I started to notice something. He started to smoke weed more than normal and not only that, he began to watch porn more than normal, mainly because I had cut him off from just about everything. No sex at all. Just did not feel like it. And because I was never his first love. His first love was marijuana, or better known as weed, sex, and pornography.
He could not go a day without it. Every time I turned around, he was firing up a blunt. It also seemed like as soon as his high would leave, there he is again firing up another one, but to him, he did not have a habit or a problem. What was even worse, he felt like he could support his habit and that was bullshit too.

Every time I turned around, he had his hand stuck out for money. Especially on my pay days and on the days, I would get child support payments. He would have his hands stuck out, looking for his part. And at first, it did not bother me, but then it became more and more prevalent he felt like I should support his habit because I was the one who always had money throughout the month. I can remember him saying to me one day, "I need to know how much money you make. We are a couple, and you see how much I make so I need to see how much you make", because abusers control people with money. And I thought to myself, "I will never show you my check stubs. That is none of your business. We are not a team and that is clearly shown in how this house runs".

I remember when my son first started working and once he got a couple of checks under his belt, he would have me to ask him for $20 here or $40 there so he could get high. Or he would ask my son could he buy food to eat for all of us. I finally put a stop to that because he was supposed to be the man. A real man does not put drugs, or anything else for that matter, before his family. A real man makes it his responsibility to make sure his family is very well taken care of. And that is one thing he never made sure of because I was the one making sure a household of 5-6 people were taken care of.

When his food stamps got cut off, much of the time, he was making sure the kids ate Little Caesar's pizza almost daily, because this was the only thing that he would pay for. Weed came first and foremost above anything and everything. Sometimes, he would give me money, but then when he would get mad, he would ask for it back. One day, he asked me why did I not ask him for money anymore and my answer to him came out just like this, "Why in the fuck am I going to ask you for money when all you are going to do is ask for it back? I should not have to ask you for shit. You should either give it to me or go pay some of the bills your damn self. If I do not have the money for what is needed, I am not going to ask you or anyone else, I will just wait for the next pay period and do it then. But I am done asking you for anything". I went from giving money, to tell him that I did not have money just so he would stop asking me for it, to completely cut him off from any more money for weed from me. It was more important for him to get high first than to deal with all the other things going on around in what was supposed to be a family. In the mornings, he would fire up a blunt and then leave. God only knows how many times he would smoke while he was at the barber shop working or how many times he would leave to go and get high. By the time the end of the day would come, he would get him a sack; smoke that all up and then back out a couple of hours later to get another sack. It was insane.

His habit was so bad; he would get weed on credit from those who would give it to him. Then, he would complain about owing money back to people who gave it to him on credit. But he complained because not only was he giving the money he owed them, he was also buying more weed on top of that. Again, it was so out of control that I refused to talk to him while he was smoking. Why? I am an asthmatic and his smoking did nothing but make it worse. So, one day, when I decided that I was going to stand up to him about this, I told him, "I will not talk to you while you are smoking. Your smoking is more important than my asthma to you, but to me, my health is more important than your smoking. When you finish smoking your blunt or whatever you are smoking, then we can have a conversation, but until then, don't say anything to me". He looked in total astonishment and amazement. I don't think any woman had stood up to him the way that I was starting to do. And every time he approached me this way, I would just simply get up and close the door or would just leave altogether. And for me, I had started to free myself of him little by little and he did not know how to handle it.

But weed was not the only thing he would spend money on. He was a huge fan of porn. He would watch it on his phone. When the boys would come home from school, Lee would be dead sleep with the TV blaring and yep, you guessed it, porn would be on. Whenever he wanted me to have sex with him, he would put on a porn movie as if we were going to re-enact what is going on in the movie. And for the most part, he never looked at me for being me, he looked at me as if I were a piece of meat. The only thing he wanted to do was bust a nut by any means necessary. And he wanted to have sex morning, noon and night if I would allow him. By the time we began to come to the end of our relationship, it was clear that I did not even want him touching me. It was repulsive and I just felt like, "UGH, GET YOUR DISGUSTING, DAMN HANDS OFF ME!"

It was so bad that I would not even look at him. It was almost like the scene from *The Color Purple*. I would just close my eyes and pray it would be over soon. He would often complain about me not looking at him or calling his name during sex like I had done in the past, and he would often ask me about it, right after he accuses me of sleeping around or seeing someone else. I would just look at him and say, "Who wants to have sex every morning and every evening? You act like I do not get tired and this is the only thing I want to do. No, I do not. I have had enough of your BS". Then just as soon as I said that, I cut him off from that as well. Maybe 3 weeks before me and my children moved out of the house and before he flipped his lid, he would often come and knock on the door to my daughter's room asking me to come into the bedroom with him and my reply would always be "NO". My thoughts would be, "Hell, just go and watch one the many porn movies you have bought, and get you a bottle of lotion or Vaseline. You got two hands, use them. Satisfy yourself on your own". I truly did not care about what he did as long as he was not doing it with me. I was getting to a point that I hated him and hate is such a strong word to use but that is how I felt. He could have gone out and paid for some or gotten some on the side, I did not care. Hell, he would always say to me, "I know I look good. I don't beg women for pussy. They give it to me with no problem. I got it like that". And I would say to him, "Shit, go and get it from those lame ass women who are just dropping their damn panties like that because I am tired of you and your shenanigans". But see, when you with someone, who all they think about is sex and porn, along with smoking, this is what you receive. A flipping sex crazed psychopath who cares about nothing but again, busting a nut, so they would not be "backed up". This is the only thing on their minds. Nothing more, nothing less! Just sex!

And then as previously mentioned throughout this chapter, there was the sex. This was yet another thing that came before me. And do not get me wrong, sex is one part of a relationship, but it is just one part, it is not the entire relationship. And our entire relationship was based on sex and why, because I never made it a requirement to be based on anything else but that.

I should have taken my time to get to know him a little bit more and better, instead of feeding my own sexual urges and desires that were never truly satisfied with him. Our sex would not last more than 20 minutes. Sometimes it would be done sooner than that. All he wanted to do was have sex. If he could have it for breakfast, lunch, and dinner, then he would. It didn't matter what time of the day it was, he wanted it and even went so far as to use a bible verse to go along with it when I did not want to or complained about it.

He would be so mad that I would not submit myself to him. Why should I have done that? Hell, I am not your wife and you are not my husband. You are someone else's husband. Here is the scripture he would fall back on. Ephesians 5:22-24 says, ***"You wives submit to your husbands as you do to the Lord. For a husband is the head of his wife as Christ is the head of his body, the church; he gave his life to be her Savior. As the church submits to Christ, so you wives must submit to your husbands in everything"***. "How in the world can you recite the above to me as you think you are holier than God"? But as it continues to state in Ephesians, Chapter 5, outside of being divorced, this what he failed to do as being the head of the house where he is not married to me, but someone else, versus 25-33 state, ***"And you husbands must love your wives with the same love Christ showed the church. He gave up his life for her, to make her holy and clean, washed by baptism and God's word. He did this to present her to himself as a glorious church without a spot or wrinkle or any other blemish. Instead, she will be holy and without fault. In the same way, husbands ought to love their wives as they love their own bodies, for a man is loving himself when he loves his wife. No one hates his own body, but lovingly cares for it, just as Christ cares for his body, which is the church. And we are his body. As the Scripture says, "A man leaves his father and mother and is joined to his wife, and the two are united into one. This is a great mystery, but it is an illustration of the way Christ and the church are as one. So again, I say, each man must love his wife as he loves himself, and the wife must respect her husband"***.

He would keep saying this to me about sex. I would find myself questioning myself like I was the one doing something wrong when it came down to sex with him. It was like I was making excuses to say why it would be okay to have sex with him, when deep down inside, I felt like and knew this was not right and I should never have been with him. So, I would make myself think that it was good, but in the back my head, I would be like, "Ugh. Sex with him sucks". It is just that simple. He could not satisfy me orally either. That was yet another thing that I had to fake, but he thought he was the bomb. Every morning, he wanted it and every night he wanted it. The only time I could keep him off me was when it was that time of the month and I would be so freaking happy about it because I would at least have some time for myself to breathe and keep him off me, for at least 5-7 days. But then, he would be right back on me and I was just miserable. I felt like I had nothing left. The children were always in their rooms with the doors closed because all he wanted to do was have sex. I would not have a lot of interaction with my own children and I could see how much of an effect it was having on the children. And then, this man would make my daughter close her door all the time because he did not believe in putting on underwear first thing in the morning. He walked through the house butt-ass naked all the damn time.

I begin to feel like something I have never, ever considered myself before. Something I knew he looked at me as. He looked at me as a piece of meat, more like a whore if anything else and I was starting to look at myself the same way because I began to say to myself "How could you let this man degrade and de-womanize you all for the sake of love? Don't you have more respect for not only yourself, but your children as well? What do you think they think about you? Do you want your daughter growing up thinking this is what love is"? And the answer to that question was, "No". And I began to have less and less sex with him to the point where it did not matter if we had sex at all and that is why he would he began to recite the Ephesian scriptures to me. He would make himself look like he was the best thing smoking, but he was a loser who truly did not know how to put anyone first but himself.

He never knew how to love anyone or anything. He never knew how to love himself. All he loved was weed, sex, and porn. As long as this was a major factor in his life, he was okay. The minute any one of these started to crumble, he would crumble. If he did not smoke, he was angry. If he did not have sex with me, he was angry. Because to him, having sex with me gave him power and control, and most if not all abusers use sex to their advantage. He could watch porn whenever, but I felt like, if it was not part of his routine, he would get mad because he wanted to watch it as he was having sex with me and I would not want to watch it let alone try to reenact a scene with him. I was so busy trying to compete for his love for the things he valued the most that I neglected my own children in the process. And I say that to say this, do I love my children? Yes, without a shadow of a doubt. However, I was so focused on his wants and needs that neglected my own children's wants and needs and they needed me to be their mother, not his mother. And I was truly a mother to everyone in the house, included a grown ass man who would throw temper tantrums when he did not get his way.

Chapter Five

Nightmare on Heatherlea Dr.

    This day will be forever sketched in my head. Everything started the night before on Saturday, 7/18/2015. It was a hot summer night. Black Expo was taking place and he wanted to enjoy some of the festivities. He wanted me to wear a dress and instead of him asking me to wear one, he basically demanded that I wore one. Looked in the closet, and instead of wearing a dress, I thought, "I would wear a nice pair of shorts, a cute top and a pair of heel and call it a night". When he came in and saw my choice of clothing, he flew off into a rage. Lee's comments were, "I thought I told you to wear a dress! If I wanted you to wear shorts, I would have said that. I don't know why we are going anywhere anyway. We ain't even talking to each other". And correct, I was not speaking to him. I had been badgered by him most, if not all the day, I had enough and I had a lot going on in mind about him. So, since we did not go out that evening, I decided to put clothes on and go bowling, all by myself. I needed some time away from everyone. After a while, I told him that I was bowling and if he wanted to talk about what bowling alley I was at? His exact text back was, "Do you". Basically, like, continue doing what you were doing because I am done. When I returned home, we still were not speaking to each other and that was fine with me. I went to bed. He kept leaving the house, of course to buy weed and whatever other drug he was using to get as high as he could.

    The next morning was Sunday, July 19, 2015. My son had to be at work. So, as I would normally do, I got up and took him to work. I stopped and got me a coffee and Lee a sweet tea and went home as my daughter and his son were still there. I walked in the door, put the coffee on the table and proceeded to give him the tea. As I was handing him the tea, he was trying to get his clothes and walk out the door, but I insisted that we talk. He did not want to and

I should have just let him leave because the events that happened after that were horrible, unimaginable to say the least.

He was trying to leave and I was pulling him to stay to make him talk because by this time I was ready to talk. I was also ready to let him know that I did not want to be in this relationship anymore and that we needed to go our separate ways. I had the cup of coffee in my hands. I was pulling on him to come back in the house and talk. As he jerked away, he jerked so hard, the coffee went flying everywhere, all of him and me. "Look at what you did! You ruined my outfit!" Hell, I did not care, because I paid for the whole damn outfit, from the shirt, to the pants and shoes. I told him, "You made me do this acting crazy". So, as he went into the house to get something to dry off with, I went in sat in the car. The car I bought and paid for. He came outside and was like, "Get out the car, I am not in the mood. You need to get out of the car". I said no. Then I remembered, I had left the other set keys in the house. He began to pull the car door open as I was trying to get out. I ran back in the house to get the other set of keys. I then ran back over to the car to still try to keep him from leaving. When I get over to the car door, he pushed me away. I proceeded to push him back. He then pushed me again, but this time as he pushed, he busted my lip in the process. I then got angry. I was mad as hell like, who does he think he is? I am going to show him". I went into the house and grabbed a large monkey wrench and came back out. Before he drove off in my car, I busted the bottom corner of the front windshield on the driver side. And that is when all hell broke loose.

As I tried to get back in the house, he literally tried to snatch me through a steel door with mesh wire. He punched the screen out and snatched me by my hair trying to pull me through the screen door. I am screaming to the top of my lungs. He let me loose and came in the house and as I am trying to get away or find something to hit him with, he began screaming, "LOOK AT WHAT YOU DID! YOU MAKE ME SICK! I HATE YOU BITCH! LOOK AT WHAT YOU DID! YOU COULD HAVE PUT MY EYE OUT! YOU

TOOK MY DADDY'S WRENCH AND BUSTED THE WINDOW, YOU STUPID BITCH! I HATE YOU! He then proceeded to spit in my face, not once, not twice but three times. By this time, I am enraged and trying to find something to smack the hell out of him with. I went into the kitchen, but he was on my heels. I went to grab a butcher knife and he said, "What are you going to do with that! If you cut me or try to stab me, I am going to KILL you!" I put the knife back and tried to get out the house. He then picked up the cup of tea and threw it all over me. And I am standing there, telling him to leave and he is like NO. He then pushed me. So, as a natural reaction and reflex, I pushed him back. He pushed me again, and this time, when he pushed me, I slipped, fell and my head bounced off the ceramic tile floor that was in the house. I instantly felt something wet running down the left side of my face.

When I rose, and he saw my face, I knew then, there was a problem. I ran to the bathroom and looked at myself and immediately started screaming. I had about a ½ inch to 1-inch gash over my left eye. I told him that he was going to take me to the emergency room. I could have driven myself to the ER, but I did not because something in me was like, if he takes me to the ER, they would arrest him on the spot because, at that point, I would have told them it was him who did this to me. However, this is not what happened. I demanded he take me to the ER. As we were in the car, driving to the ER, he continued to call me out of my name. I was everything but a child of God. I was a bitch this and whore that. "You stupid man! I hate you!" And this went on for about 3-4 minutes.

Then he turned around and spit on me again, and this time, I smacked him in the face with my open hand. I thought about picking up the monkey wrench that was in the car and smacking him the face with that or maybe crushing his nuts, but I was so scared that I left it on the floor of the car. After I smacked him in the face, he backhanded me in the mouth and busted my top lip. I then took the steering wheel and jerked it, almost causing an accident. He told me, "KEEP IT UP, YOU STUPID BITCH AND I AM NOT TAKING YOU ANYWHERE!" I jerked the wheel again, and he turned the car around and headed back to the house. As we were driving back, he hit me again in the face and took my keys and my phone. Here I am begging for both the keys to my truck and my phone. I did this all the way home. What was a 5-minute drive, seemed like hours. All I wanted to do was get to the house, get my daughter and get the hell out of there.

We made it back to the house. As we proceeded to walk in the house, I started calling my daughter's name and he said, "Why in the hell are you calling for her bitch! She ain't here. She ain't here! He then said to me again, "I HATE YOU". I had my back to him walking away, but as I am walking, I stated to him, "I HATE YOU TOO!" He then pulled me by my hair and swung me around. As I lifted my right leg to try to kick him and get him off me, he caught my leg and pulled it all the way back to my head, and the bone in my thigh popped. I screamed and he carried me to the couch. And then, like you would flip the switch to turn the lights on, he snapped out of the rage he was in. He had me sitting on his lap. "Look at us.

We need to leave each other alone. This is not my fault. You made me do this", is what he said. I got up and put pressure on my leg to make sure I could walk. I went straight to the bathroom and looked at myself in the mirror. I began to ask myself, "Just what the hell are you doing" As I started to wipe my face, I noticed blood at the top of my left ear. That is when I found out, I had another gash behind my left ear, but I did not know how big, deep or long it was because I could not see it. Then he comes behind me, "Let me put some peroxide on it". "NO! DO NOT TOUCH ME! I will drive myself to the ER".

I found my keys and phone and proceeded to get in my truck. I did not know where his son had taken my daughter, but I knew she was safe with him. It was later determined; he took her to the park because she was scared and did not want to be in the house anymore. Lee was like, "What are you doing? I will take you and drop you off and I am leaving". I just kept walking. Once I got in the truck, I immediately locked the doors and drove off. I called my sister and by this time, I was screaming and in a state of shock as to what had just transpired. Once I got off the phone with her, I called my father.

I told him what happened and he stayed on the phone with me until I made it to the ER. I was still somewhat scared because I did not know if Lee was following me or what, but one thing was for sure, I was not stopping until I made it to the ER. I pulled up to the ER while still on the phone with my father. Once inside, he asked me to give the phone to the receptionist and I did. He proceeded to let her know what happened to me and her exact words to him were, "She is with us and she is in a safe place and we will take excellent care of her. No one can hurt her here". The nurse receptionist put me in the triage room and before I could sit down, the ER doctor and sheriff's deputies were coming to take me to a secure treatment room.

Unknowingly to me, my sister called my uncle. As I am letting the physician know what transpired, my uncle walked in the room. I remember stating to him, "Look at my face", as I sat there in tears. The next two people that came into the room were the forensic nurse and an IMPD officer. He asked me about the events that had just transpired and I told him everything. He asked me what should happen to Lee because at this point he is going to jail. I did not care what they did with him. I did not want him in my presence. He has turned my life completely upside down. The forensic nurse began to take pictures of my injuries.

From the busted lips to the bruises where he pinched and twisted my arm until it turned purple, the gash behind my ear and the one over my eye. I was bruised and bloodied from head to toe. She left me with a packet of information that I would need. She also informed me that Child Protective Services (CPS) may be contacting me regarding my daughter and this was standard procedure. The only thing I kept thinking was, "Oh my God, CPS is going to take my children away from me. What have I done "? and started to cry even more. The police officer sent out units to apprehend Lee. My uncle stayed with me at the emergency room. The physician's assistant came in to look at my injuries because I was getting stitches. It was determined I would need 4 stitches over my eye and 6 behind my ear. He decided to numb the area behind my ear first. I was 42 at the time of all this had transpired and I was lying on the table screaming like a new born baby. There were 2 additional nurses in the room. One had to hold my ear down while the PA numbed it with lidocaine. The other nurse was there for support and held my hand and told me if I needed to squeeze her hand through the pain, I could and that everything would be okay. And that is what I did.

Once I was all stitched up, I followed my uncle back to his house. I was so happy to see my baby girl that all I could do was to hold her and cry. His son was there also. I went upstairs and laid down. I laid staring up at the ceiling trying to grasp what just happened, and the phone rings. "Hello". I wish I would have never answered the phone. I should have just let it ring. But nope, like a dummy I answered. It was Lee. "Janea, I am so sorry. You know I love you and I would never do anything to hurt you. This is not my fault. If you had not pushed me, none of this would have ever happened". It was at that very moment that I snapped. I replied to him, "So I caused myself to get 10 stitches. I caused myself to spit on myself. I caused me to get pulled through a steel door. I busted my lips in two places on my own.

How in the world could I have done all of this to myself and you not have anything to do with it, but you were the other participant! Stop calling me! I have nothing to say to you at all!" And hung the phone up. And he calls right back. His words went something like, "Please listen to me. I love you too much to want to hurt you". My statement back to him "What the fuck ever!" "Stop calling me!" and I proceeded to hang up on him yet again. He just kept calling and I finally turned the ringer off.

So here I was. My mind was racing, going a million miles a minute. I could not figure out anything. I was so hurt and in a lot of pain. The anesthesia was starting to wear off and my leg was beginning to hurt too. I just laid in the bed and cried, and cried, and cried. I just wanted to go into a corner or closet and wither away. I constantly kept asking myself, "How could you have let this happen? How could you have let things get this bad"? And the only answer I could remotely come up with was, I did not listen to God. God was giving me all the signs of this man being unstable, but I just refused to listen.

      My uncle and aunt went to pick my son up from work. When he got home, he immediately came upstairs and looked at me and just gave me hug. I cried again. We then had to go back to the house and get clothes for the next day. Went home and got clothes and started heading back to my uncle's house. The phone rings and guess who it is, again! Yep, you guessed it, Lee. "Let me talk to my son" is all he kept saying. But instead of him talking to his son, my son was the one who he talked to. "How could you do this to my mom? Why did you put your hands on my mother? She did not deserve any of this from you". And in true Lee fashion, his response was, "Do you believe everything your mother and others say to you"? And my son replied to him, "This is my mother. I will ALWAYS believe my mother over you. Even if she told me to lie, I would still believe her because she is my mom". My son then told him, "If you want to speak to your son, call him on the phone he has. Stop calling my mom's phone". We finally made it back to the house and he just kept calling and again the phone went on silent.

Chapter Six

Victim vs. Victim

So now the fun begins. I was truly a victim of my environment and victim of my circumstance. I kept asking myself, "How did I let this happen"? I had become a Battered Woman (BW) and I was suffering from Battered Woman's Syndrome (BWS). I couldn't tell you if I was coming or going. I was just existing, trying to come to grips with what had just happened to me. And the worst part, all of this happened about 3 weeks prior to me having major surgery and my parents were in the process of packing up their home in Gary and moving to Las Vegas. Yeah, I was a complete mess. And he would not stop calling me. Every time he called it was something new.

Finally, the No Contact order was put into the place on that Monday, 7/20/15. And he could no longer call me because if he did, the charges would be worse. Our first court date was on that Wednesday, 7/23/2015. I will never forget it. I went to this court date on my own. No one accompanied me as I needed to face him on my own. Upon entering, I met with the Victim's Assistance Advocate. Once I made it into her office, I just began to cry and would not stop crying. I remember her telling me this, "Do not let him see you cry. If he sees you crying, he is going to try everything to get you to help get him out of jail. Do not let him see you are upset and scared. I will be there with you". And after waiting for 4 hours, we finally had our initial hearing. He expected me not to show up. He expected me not to be there, but I was there. Stitches over my eye, which were covered with butterfly sterile strips and 6 stitches behind my ear. He is sitting there with his court-appointed attorney, wanting to say, "I cannot believe she actually showed up". You are damn right I did. This needed to be recorded somewhere in the justice system.

    The prosecutor began to read the charges and as she read them, I began to get angry. Mad as hell. The judge watched me the entire time. I would not even look at Lee. I was outdone. I did not know what to do. As his defense attorney was pleading for his release, I was praying for him to stay behind bars, because I had not had any peace and at the time, this was the only peace I had. I remember the judge asking me about the no contact order and if it was not in place, would he contact me. "Yes, Your Honor, he would". I knew that him not being from this state and he did not have anyone else in his corner that lived here. So, she kept the no contact order valid. He could not even call his son. I was so thrilled because that meant I could have some peace as I try to figure out what to do. But that was short lived.

    He was released 24 days on GPS monitoring, on or around August 12, 2015, and who did he call first me. "I need you to bring me the keys and the car". "The car has a busted window and you do not need to drive it". But the question I should have been asking myself is, "Why in the world are you having a conversation with this man? The same man who left you with these injuries. The same man who spit on you. The same man who busted your lip. Why on earth are you talking or even engaging in a conversation with him"? And the only answer I could come up with was, I was truly suffering from BWS. I had suffered from the bullshit for so long, I could not walk away from it. All I knew at that point in time was chaos. I could not detach away from it. And what was even worse, not only did I pay his bail (with his debit card), I also picked him up as he was walking away from Marion County Community Corrections (MCCC), coming down West Washington St. And we hugged as if nothing had happened. To gain a better and clearer understanding of what I was suffering from, I am going to give the definition of BWS.

Battered Woman Syndrome

The set of symptoms, injuries, and signs of mistreatment seen in a woman who has been repeatedly abused by a spouse, partner or relative.

Another name and definition states it as the following:

Battered Person Syndrome
A physical and psychological condition of a person who has suffered (usually persistent) emotional, physical or sexual abuse from another person.

And any way you looked at it, I suffered from both. And therefore, I could not walk away at that time. I could not even convince myself that I was abused. I was always making excuses for him and what he had done to me. I was always second guessing myself.

When he was first released from jail, we stayed overnight in a hotel room. He did not want to talk about the incident that night he just wanted to be with me. But I was stupid and blinded by love that I did not even think about the fact of what he had just done to me 24 days prior. All I cared about was being around him. Talk about stupid. Yeah, you could have written that across the top of my forehead and I would not have even cared. At that time and in my mind, it felt good to be wanted. The bad part of all of this was the feeling of not being wanted; it was being wanted by a no-good fraction of a man, rather an abuser, who never gave a damn about me. And I think, once he was released, is when he made his decision to seek and destroy, not rebuild and repair.

He could not afford to stay in the hotel anymore, so he had to stay with a mutual family friend and his family. And at the same time, my parents were in town. They had sold their house and stayed in Indy for a week. They were also here because I was getting ready to have major surgery. But for Lee, because he could not see his son, he felt like I should not see my family. He also felt like because it was my fault that he was jailed for 24 days, I should be at his beck and call. And again, like a damn dummy, I was. If he wanted something to eat, here I go running like a chicken with my head cut off getting it. Then he would constantly call me. I would walk away from everyone just to talk with him. I was hiding away more from everyone just to salvage what I thought I wanted with him. Boy, was I wrong! I wish I would have taken his son back to Nashville, so there would be nothing to tie us together but the court. But I did not.

I had surgery and stayed overnight in the hospital. I found myself calling him once I was out of surgery, but he never answered the phone. I called like two or three times. By the next morning, I was up and moving around and preparing to leave to go home. I found myself calling him again trying to talk with him. Then he finally answered and said, "I saw that you were calling me, but I don't understand why you did not call yesterday before you went to the hospital". Wait, what the hell? I could not believe he just said that to me. It was then followed up with, "You were so wrong for that and it really hurt my feelings that you did not even call me before you went into surgery. You left my son at the house by himself and did not care if he had anything to eat or cared if he was safe".

Then, I fired back, "You knew I was having surgery and my mind was not on calling you, it was on me. Making sure that I was going to be okay! Making sure my children were safe. I told you the night before, you needed to have someone come and get your son from the house because he would be there by himself, yet you chose not to. So, don't come putting that BS off on me. He is your son and your responsibility". I would later come to find out, our friend's wife asked him if he would like for her to pick John up and he could have stayed the night with him at their home but he told her no.

As I continued to recover at home, he continued to bug the hell out of me and have me running all over the place. When I would say no, he would pout like a fucking baby. Then he discovered he could video call me via Facebook. Every night, he would call me on that damn FB video chat, trying to see what was I doing and repeating over and over, "I just want to come home to my bed and family". He would not stop. Along with that, he kept begging me to get him off GPS monitoring. He kept laying his guilt at my doorstep about him being on house arrest.

One day when I went to see him, he was all in his feelings. "You told everyone about what happened. You made yourself look good, while I look like an ass. You never told them about what you did or when you smacked me in the face and hit me in the nose. Then you went and talked with another person. Why were you talking to them? Why was he calling you and what did he want? Are you messing around with him"? He was so insecure and he just knew I was messing around with someone else. After listening to him whine, bitch, gripe and complain, I finally exited out of my vehicle and walked away. I could not take any more of the BS he was talking about. He acted like I was at fault for everything that happened and he was defending himself against me. I walked into a local restaurant to get something to drink and here he comes. "I am sorry. It is just that I want to be at home with you and the kids".

During this time, I had to get the window repaired on the car. Well, of course, the day I am set to get it repaired, he is calling me because let's remember now, it was my fault from the beginning. "That this is all the transportation I have. I am going to meet you at the car place". He never offered to help get the window repaired! I paid for it out of my pocket. And if he was mobile, he did not care. We had an argument on that same day and then I tuned him out. I would not say anything to him. I had our friend take me to my truck so I could go to work. Then the weekend came around. We had an argument about something and I told him about himself yet again. "It is because of you that I did 24 days in jail.

How would you feel if you had to go to jail for something that was not your fault"? My response, "I do not give a fuck about you spending 24 days in jail. When my head bounced off the ceramic floor, I could have died on the spot. My children could have been motherless and my parents would have had to bury their daughter. I did not cause this mess. You did. You were so enraged and filled with hate, that all you could see was hurting me. You are depressed about your father passing, but refuse to get help. You act as if you are the only person on this earth who has lost a parent. You need some help with your anger issues too. But let me help you to understand, I don't give a damn about the 24 days you have done when my life could have been taken". There was dead silence on the phone.

It was time for him to head back to court. By this time, I was not the same person. Although I stood my grounds on some things with us, on other things, I felt weak and intimidated by him. When we went back, it was to determine if he should be taken off GPS. His guilt influenced my decision on having him released from GPS and the case being continued. I sat in court and the judge asked me did I fear for my safety with him, "No". I replied. "We had an argument that got way out of control. It should have never gotten to that point". And just that quick, it was over.

He was off GPS. The no contact order was lifted and he could return to the house that I now considered the "house of horrors". He went out and bought balloons and flowers for me and a stuffed animal for my daughter. He bought his son's shoes. But it was my son who did not take it well at all. "Mom, what is he doing here? Why is here? Are you all getting back together? No mom, not after what he did to you. Please tell me no". I could not even look at my son with a straight face. I felt like such an idiot. I let my children down, but what's even worse, I let me down. I knew I should not have gotten back with him. I knew it was wrong, but I did not want to be lonely and by myself, so I chose to try to make amends with him instead of leaving him alone. It would turn out to be the 2nd worst mistake I had ever made in this lifetime because the 1st mistake was having a relationship with him to begin with. The fight I was fighting did not belong to me, it belonged to God. It was like I was having a battle with God and the Devil but in the end, I ALWAYS knew God would prevail.

Every day it was the same old thing with him. "Let me see how I can put more guilt on her shoulders about me being locked up for something that was her fault", is what I felt like was going through his head. If it was not, "You kept me away from my son for 24 days", it was "Do you know what it's like to have your freedom taken from you"? Or it would be, "My father has died and you do not even care. You are not compassionate at all. You do not know what it is like to lose your parents. Hell, your parents are still walking. My father is dead and is not coming back". The best one of his victim statements was this, "How could you compare the loss of your daughter that lived for an hour to the loss of my father that I had for 38 years"? That was the one that hit the hammer on the nail. It was all about him. It was all about his feelings. It was all about making me look like a liar and a bad person to others while he tries to maintain the good guy image. And I was not the only person that he inflicted this on.

On Memorial Day of 2015, he was dead set on going with me over to my uncle's house. In his mind, since my uncle and aunt did not side with him on the incident that happened in August of 2012. He wanted to make himself look like a victim as well. As we sat outside talking with my uncle and aunt, he started talking about that incident in general. "You all were wrong. You did not even help me when my children needed somewhere to go, but you all (my uncle and aunt) were quick to take her children in". And I thought to myself, "Are you serious? Is this what this is all about? However, my uncle's reply was, "No disrespect. This is about blood and she is my blood and I will always be there for her whether she is wrong or right". He was mad as hell because he wanted someone, anyone to be on his side. But there are no sides in right vs. wrong. It is and will always be, right is right and wrong is wrong. Not who will stand with you and try to make the other person look bad.

And as we all sat there and listened to his whining and pining, my aunt casually says to him, "Oh, you are the victim, right? Nothing happens to anyone else but you. No one has had a significant loss but you". Then he was fuming. "Do you have both of your parents"? My aunt simply replied, "Yes, I do. But I have lost both a sister and brother that I was very close to and it was a significant loss to my family and I". My uncle replied, "I have lost my mother. I know what it is like to lose a parent". Do you think Lee heard that? No, because it was not about him, nor did it affect him.

What I learned is that most, if not all people who are narcissists or have narcissistic tendencies, only care about making themselves look good to others in public, while in private, they are making your life, along with immediate household family members' lives hell. And as time went on, I was about to learn just how much more difficult it was going to become.

Chapter Seven

The Big Setback

"What in the world are you thinking "? is what I kept asking myself, as we tried to settle back into a routine that was far from normal. There was not anything normal about what was happening. Lives had been shattered and torn apart. But somewhere along the way, we tried to make it seem like it was all going to work and we were going to get help as a couple. There was one problem with that, I was the only one getting help. I was the only one who tried to make things work. He did not give a damn about making things work. He cared about other things, but not this relationship. So why was I fighting to save something that I should have let go when he was incarcerated? Simply put, I refused to see what others saw. I did not want to believe that we were over (although it was over before it even began).

I remember before getting out of the car and going to my counseling session, I was on the phone talking with my dad. "Janea, how could you be with someone who did all of the things that he did to you and think that it is okay? I would not want to be near anyone who spits on me". As I continued to sit and listen to my dad's voice, I began to cry because he was right. How could I do that? I could not even begin to answer the question. Everyone was so ashamed of me and most importantly, I was ashamed and embarrassed with myself. People who were the closest to me never judged me, but continued to be concerned about me and my well-being. They only wanted what was best for me and my children. I also remember having a conversation with his brother, rather his best friend. "Janea, if you are not going back like you say you are not, then you must stand your ground and not go back. But do not tell people you are not going back and you end up going back. That is not a good look".

And he was so right. I wish I would have listened to him, but everyone else as well.

No sooner than he was released and taken off house arrest than the madness started back up. This would now be September 2015. His eldest son had moved back to TN and his youngest was still living there with us. Both his son and my son were gone, off to school and it was just me and my daughter there alone with him. He woke up in a funk as always. I cannot even remember what we were arguing about. I had just gotten out of the shower. My daughter was getting ready to take a shower and here he comes down the hall, with no clothes on. "Get out the bathroom! You and your mama always in the bathroom taking up too much time and I am the last one in the bathroom! Janea, you need to make her take her showers at night!" "Why? To appease you? She is a little girl and she can take a shower after me if she wants. She is fine". I said to him, "I was wondering when the old you was going to show back up. Everything you said you were not going to do, you are doing and doing more of". And it went from there. He was coming up behind me to the bedroom. And as we are arguing, he slams the door. I am over by the dresser trying to get some underwear out of the drawer, as all I had on was a towel.

Not only did he snatch the towel off me, every time I pulled out a pair of underwear out of the drawer, he snatched them out of my hand. "Stop, let me get dressed! I need to get ready for work and she needs to get for school and we are going to be late". Before I knew it, in a fit of rage, he knocks everything off the dresser, included the jewelry box that belonged to my grandmother that was over 20 plus years old. I started walking towards the door and he runs around me and slams the door shut and knockouts the lotion I had in my hand. I went and sat on the bed because I began to get frustrated. And there he is, standing over me, screaming to the top of his lungs. "MOVE! GET FROM OVER ME!" "No, I am not moving", is what he kept yelling. "It is your fault that I was in jail. Had you just left me alone, this would not have happened to me".

I fell back on the bed and he kept hovering and standing over me. I raised my leg to kick him off me and he grabbed my ankle and damn near twisted it with his bare hands. "Oh, you are trying to kick me bitch!" I replied, "I am trying to get you off me and leave me alone, so we (me and my daughter) can get dressed and leave". And for the next 5-10 minutes, he kept terrorizing me. Then suddenly, there was a knock on the bedroom door. It was my daughter. "Daddy, it is me. You said that you would not do this anymore around me. Please stop arguing with mommy. It is scaring me". She was crying hard and fast. Then, like as if nothing happened, he stopped. Again, like a switch had been flipped. It was just not normal and you would have thought that would have been enough. But nope, it was not.

  Once I made it home from work, "Janea, can we talk"? And here he goes on apologizing like nothing had happened. As he continued to talk, it was clear, he was the victim in all of this. He never accepted responsibility for anything that happened and furthermore, everyone was to blame for his misfortune. All I did was to listen. I did not say anything to him at all as I did not have anything to say. I had to find a way to get out of his presence, away from him, period. It was on that day, that I had become emotionally detached from him. I was numb to all his bullshit. I knew what to expect and how it would go down because it went down like that almost daily.

  I was letting everyone down. Most importantly, I was letting me down. But I did not care at that moment. As time went on, I was constantly reminded as to why I should have never gotten back with him. He was the victim. And in his eyes, he was the one who had been betrayed. He did not believe in right is right and wrong is wrong. He believed in taking sides and if you did not take his side, you were on the wrong side. Also, if others did not take his side, he would find ways to badger them as well. "How could you believe her over me"? is what he asked one person. Every day it was something different but always the same outcome.

  By this time, it was October 2015. The lease was up on the house we lived in back in August, but because I did not have a plan B, I opted to month-to-month until I found something. Let's not forget, he was still there at this time as well. I had started planning an escape from him. I had found an apartment to move me and the kids into that a friend of mine told me about. I went to inquire about the apartment as my friend and her family lived there too and had shown me around. Feeling a sense of security, I went ahead and made the deposit and even got a move in date. "Janea, my client told me they saw you over in Wellington Village Apartments.

What is going on over there"? I never answered his question, I just blew it off as it was nothing, but I knew in the back of my head, I could not move us over there. He had several clients who lived there and they would have told him that we were there and that would have been detrimental to both me and my children and I was not about to place them in harm's way yet again or have them in a situation where I was not home and something would happen to them because he is trying to find me. So, since that was shot out the window, I had to find yet another place for us to live. I did not want them to move with us, however, I felt like I had no choice but for them to move with us because every move I would make, he was on it.

He was always asking a thousand and one questions about what I am doing or where I was going. Who I was friends with and why am I friends with them. In other words, he was trying to keep me away from anyone and everyone who would be able to help me. And he basically wanted others to alienate me so I would not have anyone. He knew outside of my parents, the only other people I truly had were my uncle and aunt. Friends would not call, they would not come and visit as they knew what type of person he was and no one, not even my uncle, aunt and my own kids wanted to be around him. He just made life unbearable. I also felt like I had no choice because he was a bully.

He would threaten me all the time about the car I bought. "I am taking this car and there is nothing you can do about it". Or in another instance, it was, "I need half of the money back on the Cadillac because that was my car was mine and you used it to trade it in to get the Charger". But hell, both cars were in my name and they were both mine. So how could you tell me what you were not going to let me keep a car that was mine? He did that because he was a bully and this is how he would try to get his point across. He was very intimidating as well and sometimes, rather most times, I would rather just give in versus fighting with him about anything. And I was also ready to just give up because I felt like it was not going to get better. It was only going to get worse. And again, we had both agreed that we did not need to be together, but I did not want to be alone and he did not either. So here we go yet again, listening to the Devil and not God. We should have never moved into another house together, but that is exactly what happened.

Mid October, we found another house. It had four bedrooms and looked nice, or so it seemed. We went and talked with the owner of the home. Since I had the verifiable income, the lease went in my name. Lee was there and he kept pressuring the landlord to add his name to the lease and just like that, he did. The funny part, he did not help to pay the deposit. Of course, that was all me. I found out later down the line, he did not want to add him to the lease at all. I will come back to this later in another chapter.

So, on November 1, 2015, we moved into this new house. He paid to get it painted. But he wanted me to pay for the moving truck and everything else. "No. I am not paying for a moving truck or van. I just spent $995 getting us into this damn house and I am not spending another damn dime. You find someone to do it or you get the truck your damn self". So, what does he do, calls one of his clients who just so happens to have his own moving truck to help us move. However, in the true negotiator fashion, he only paid him $60 cash and then smoked about 4-5 blunts with him. However, he made sure he did not do a lot of heavy lifting. He made my son and his son do most of that. All he cared about was getting high. He would not even come back and help clean out the other house. He did not help do anything really, just give orders, like we were slaves and he was the master.

There were certain things that needed to be fixed and then certain things that we would have to fix on our own. The bathroom was horrible and I wish I would have seen it before the lease was signed. You could tell that someone tried to paint the tub, but was unsuccessful with it. And although it was clean, I did not want to be there. Then, as the weather started to change, the furnace started to give out. I remember one night. I was trying to get the furnace to work. Lee was there, but of course, he was upstairs smoking. I came back upstairs frustrated. I called the landlord, and that is when I found out, all he wanted was someone to be in the house so he could be paid for it. He could have given a damn about what needed to be repaired. I could not get him on the phone and it was one of the coldest nights of the month. I was so frustrated. Lee looked at me. "Well, what's wrong with it"? is what he asked me. "How in the fuck am I supposed to know what is wrong with the furnace. I am not a man and nor do I repair furnaces. Hell, that is what you are here for and you need to figure it out".

As I am saying this, I had my daughter put her coat on and off to Walmart we went to buy heaters for the rooms just in case the furnace went completely out. Came back home and plugged one of the heaters up in my daughter's room and the power went out, in her room and on one side of the house. "Lord, what in the hell have I gotten myself into"? is what I thinking. "This house is a death trap". That was on Friday. That Saturday, the furnace repair man came out. There was another part that was needed. He said, "This is only going to last for so long". "Well, call the landlord and let him know as this is home and he is responsible for fixing this, not me". Needless to say, it never got fixed. I truly felt like I was stuck. I signed a lease for a year with a man who is an asshole. "How do I get out of this mess without him knowing about it? How can I begin to fix what I have created? I should have never, ever gone back down this path", is all I could keep thinking to myself. I was miserable and although I was attending weekly counseling sessions, I was depressed as hell because I failed myself.

It was coming up on Thanksgiving, Thanksgiving 2015 to be exact, and things were not getting any better. In fact, they continued to get worse. I did not have a chance to get Thanksgiving dinner, because, of course, I did not have any money. Outside of making him pay half of the rent, I was paying all the remaining bills. I was truly robbing Peter to pay Paul. So, I had to rely on him to get thanksgiving dinner. The pastor's wife of the church we attended just happened to call me a week before Thanksgiving and said she had a turkey to give us. She brought the turkey over and this idiot says, "I am not eating that turkey from them". "Why"? I asked. It was because the pastor did not take "his side" when he first abused me. The pastor took the side of right versus wrong and he held a grudge against him for it. "Something is wrong with you. You do not have to eat it. We will".

  He looked at me like I had three heads. Then I asked him would he go to the grocery store and get the remainder of what we needed for Thanksgiving dinner. He bitched, griped and complained. "You said you would have money. I thought you were getting paid. That is what you told me". "My paycheck did not hit as expected or I would have gone myself. I don't like asking you to do a damn thing because you make a big deal about it". "Well, you need to give me some money when you get paid". "No. I will not because I feed this damn family all the fucking time. This is the least you could do outside of feeding them those damn Little Caesar's pizzas every time we need to eat". He was mad as hell and I did not give two shits about him being mad either.

  Thanksgiving Day came and went. The next day, my paycheck hit and I had to go and wash clothes because the washer was out. Later that day, when I got home, I began to have an asthma attack. Do you think he made it a point to take me to the doctor or to Urgent Care? Hell, no. My son, his sons and my daughter took me to Urgent Care. He stayed at the house and you guessed it, smoked a fucking blunt. This would be the 2nd asthma attack I would have that he did not take me to the ER or a doctor. The first one was in May of 2014. I drove myself to the ER, praying I would not have a severe attack. "I was on my way up there, but you all got back before I could make it up there". I just looked at him, and did not say one word and thought to myself, "You pathetic bastard". I was infuriated. However, the next turn of events was truly the deal-breaker.

Chapter Eight

The Nightmare Continues

As we continued with this façade for others that everything was alright, it was falling apart and falling apart fast. By this time, we had been in this death trap of a house for a little over a month, going on two months. It was going on Christmas. I was still broke and trying to figure out how I was going to buy gifts for the kids and pay bills all at the same time. It was so bad that I did not even put up a Christmas tree and did not give a damn about Christmas that year. The only thing Lee was paying was half of the rent. I was trying to pay my half of the rent, electric bill, gas/water bill, cable/internet/phone bills, buy groceries, pay 2 car notes and do Christmas shopping all at the same time and I was wearing myself thin.

He then came to me and said, "Well, I have half of the car note money. You can put the other half with it and at least it would be paid". "The car note is now 3 months behind and sending them ½ of a payment is not going to do anything because I am not paying anything towards the car. You are going to have to pay at least 1 full car payment". "I am not going to do that. That will leave me with no money and I am not going to be broke", was his response and that was primarily because, it would take away from the weed he smoked, day in and day out. So, my decision, I was not going to pay it and I did not.

Later in the week, he was talking about he had a conversation with our mutual friend's wife (the same mutual friend that allowed him to stay with his family while he was on GPS monitoring). They were talking about cars and car notes. In casual conversation, she had mentioned her husband was upset about her not wanting to pay for something. And her response to him was something like, "Why should I pay for something that is not mine"? So, guess who took on that same mentality? Yep, you guessed it. Lee. We were talking about paying bills and the car came up. His basic response, "Shit, why am I going to pay for something that is not mine"? Little did he know; those same words would come back to bite him in the ass. I looked at him like, "Are you serious? This is a joke, right"? "I am not driving the Charger or the Explorer anymore. Those are both your cars. You bought them, you pay for them". "I bought the Charger for you so you would have a decent car to drive. You agreed to pay the car note. Why in the hell would I want 2 car payments "? was my reply to him. He just looked at me blank faced because he was not going to pay for the car.

One day, while I was sitting at my desk at work, I was just trying to brainstorm on how to get out of this huge amount of debt I had gotten myself into. I talked with a former coworker regarding who she used for her bankruptcy. She gave me the name and number for the attorney, because I was so far in debt, at any moment, the repo man was coming to pick up the both vehicles. I made an appointment to meet with the bankruptcy attorney and decided on that day in December 2015, that I was going to file another Chapter 7. Wipe the slate clean and start over. When I got home, later that evening, this is how the conversation played out and boy he was pissed. "I met with a bankruptcy attorney today. I am filing bankruptcy. I am wiping the slate clean and everything is going back. That includes both the car and the truck because you are right, why should you pay for something that is not yours". Lee's response, "You did not even talk this over with me. If we are a couple, you should have told me first instead of doing this and not talking to me". "I am not married to you and we do not own anything together.

Wasn't it you who said and I quote, "Why should I pay for something that is not mine"? And you are so right. You should not have to pay for anything that does not belong to you. So, both vehicles go back". He was mad as hell. "When are they coming to pick up the car? How am I supposed to get back and forth to work"? "They are not coming anytime soon and until they do, you can drive it, but I would strongly suggest you start saving money because you are going to need a car and I am not funding another vehicle or anything for you or anyone else". "Well, you traded in the Cadillac to get the Charger and that was my car". "Correction, Lee that was my car. Remember, it was in my name due to at the time, you did not even have a driver's license. I could do what I wanted to do with that car". No matter what, I continued with my plan of action to file bankruptcy and did not give a flying flip about what he thought or how he felt. So, then he continued to nag the hell out of me about that. I was like, "You sound like a whining ass baby. SHUTUP!"

    Christmas came. No tree. Barely any presents. My son and his son got money and hoodies. My daughter got clothes and a few toys, but not much. I did not have any money to buy anything. It was by far the worst Christmas me and my children ever experienced. Then, even on that day, things were awful. Someone called Lee for a haircut on Christmas day. And you guessed it, he went. Why? He needed money for weed. I was so angry. I let the kids open their gifts. Hell, it wasn't like they had much anyway and they all knew it. So, when he came back from the barber shop, of course, he was on one because I let them open their gifts without him. "Why did you let them do that without me being here"? "Well, if Christmas was so important and you wanted to see them open their gifts, you would have stayed here to see it.

    Frankly, I could give a damn if you saw them open the gifts or not". And then he went on and on about that. So later that day, I posted a pic of me and the kids (my son and daughter) on FB for holidays with the statement, "Happy Holidays from my Family to Yours". Then the fireworks flew. "Everyone is calling telling me about the pic you posted and you did not include me and my son. Your definition of family is really messed up Janea". I just looked at him. Then this is what followed, "You can't possibly think this is a family? We do not function or act like a family. Everyone is on their own page, doing their own thing", and it just kept going on and on and on, all day.

I was also in the process of completing a research paper for my English class. Well, I decided to do my research paper on Domestic Violence, because now I had been victimized by it. It was late on a Sunday night and I had to have the first rough draft turned in that night. "What are you in here working on? It is late and you have been on this computer off and on all day. You have not paid any attention to me". "Just go away", were my thoughts, but my response was, "I am completing my first draft for my research paper". "What are you researching"? is the question he asked while he was rolling up a blunt for the umpteenth time that day. "I am doing my research paper on Domestic Violence". Domestic Violence! Did you say Domestic Violence"? "Yes, I did. I did not stutter about it. You heard me correctly". He walked away and smoked his blunt. He had a look of both disbelief and shock because I think he thought I was going to mention what happened with us earlier in the year. However, I wanted to know more about why women who had been victims of abuse continued to go back to the person or persons who had abused them. I also was still trying to figure a way out of this horror story I was in and this was a good way to do both. I was slowly but surely getting out of my own way and listening to God and not man.

We entered January 2016. Same shit, new year. Since we did not have any living room furniture, I had a lot of my things in the living room. "You need to move your stuff into the room. How is it going to look when people come to visit and you have all your things in the living room? And we are a couple and we do not need to be living like this. Let's work on doing right". So, to keep the peace, I proceeded to move my things back into the bedroom. But that did not last long. The arguments continued. One day, it was brutally cold outside and his son and my son got up to get ready for school. Well, his son went ahead and walked to school as the school was only five-to-ten minutes away. My son decided not to walk and waited for me to give him a ride. "Do you think you are too good to walk to school? My son walked, why didn't you walk"? My son replied, "Because it is cold and I did not want to walk". Then here we go. He got mad with the answer and was going to try to fight my son. I immediately jumped up getting in between them. "Janea, you better say something to him, because his smart-ass mouth is going to cause him to get beat down by me". "I WILL DIE FOR MY CHILDREN. I WILL LEAVE YOU BEFORE YOU PUT YOUR HANDS ON THEM AND YOU WILL NOT HAVE ANYTHING! TRUST AND BELIEVE THAT!"

Then after all of that, he turned right around and took my son to school and then came back to the house to terrorize me about what happened because I stood behind my son and had my son's back and not his. "You are letting these kids come between us. You are supposed to have my back and not his". What the hell? He could not have been serious. "Those are my children and not yours and it is about time that I put them before you. For the past 4 years, I have allowed you to come in between my relationship with them. I have allowed you to come in between relationships and alienate me from everyone else as well". One a Sunday in January in 2016, we got into a heated argument in front of my daughter.

I was everything but a child of God. I was a bitch this, bitch that. "You can do for everyone else, but cannot do for me. You make me sick". "Oh, so this how you are going to talk to me in front her, really"? He apologized to my daughter as she sat there in silence. We took him to the house and left. "With tears rolling down her face, she uttered these words, "Mommy, I cannot do this anymore. Mommy, he scares me and I am scared he is going to hurt you and me. Mommy, can we move? "Yes, baby, we can. Mommy is working on it. I am not going to let him hurt you or your brother. I promise".

This is where the beginning of the end started. On January 28, 2016, he dropped me off at work. By this time, the Explorer had been repossessed as part of the bankruptcy and at the advisement of my attorney. The work day went on as normal. Then about 3:45, I got a call from Lee asking me if the police had called and my answer to him was no. About 15 to 20 minutes later, I received another phone call from him and it went something like this, "Janea, we had a car accident. We (him and my daughter) are okay. We were hit down the passenger side of the car by a school bus. I drove away from the scene. She is shaken up. I checked her over and she is fine. Can you find a ride home because I am scared and I am not sure if someone got the license plate number"? I instantly got a headache, three times over. I could barely even say anything.

All I could think about was my daughter and how scared she must have been and if she was hurt. I called one of my co-workers. She had left work for the day. I explained to her what happened and asked her, if possible, could she return and pick me up and take me home. She said it would not be a problem. I then proceeded to call another co-worker, because, by this time, my blood pressure was past ten. I told her what had just taken place and I needed someone to talk with as I was at a total loss for words. As we talked and she calmed me down, an incoming call was coming through. It was Lee. "What is taking you so long to get home? Do you need me to come and get you"? "HELL NO! I do not want you to come and pick me up. Didn't you just say you were scared to drive? I will be there when I get there!"

By the time I got home, it was dark. I could see some of the damage to the car and he was sitting in the car looking like a sitting duck. I went into the house and checked on my daughter to make sure she was okay. "Can you tell mommy what happened today"? "Mommy, we were behind a school bus and the stop sign was out from the bus. He was rushing like always. Then when the bus driver let the stop sign down, he tried to drive around the bus, but they did not see us, and they hit the side of the car, and we drove off". I was horrified, to say the least. They could have been killed. "Did he rush off because he had something on him"? "I think so mommy, but I really do not know".

He came in. "Can we talk"? I went into the living room and sat in a chair. Here is how the conversation went. "Let me say this. I am glad no one was seriously hurt. She could have been killed, you could have been killed or you both could have seriously been hurt". Then I went in. "What the hell were you thinking? You were in that much of rush that you had to drive around a school bus? And this car is not registered in your name. It is my name. If the police come, they are coming for me, not you. And how are you going to fix this? This is the 3rd car of mine you have torn up. All of this for some weed? Are you serious"? Then he got mad and lashed out at me for the accident and tried to make it seem like it was my fault. Now here comes the victim. "You make it seem like it was you involved in the accident. It was me. I could have been hurt. I know you were not driving and if the police come to the house, I will let them know it was me. I will not let you take the fall for this. And we need to try to find someone to fix it. I will pay for all of it out of my tax money I get from Child Support. You are worried about the wrong thing".

 I looked up at the ceiling and said: "Lord am I getting punk'd? I think I am getting punk'd. Where are the cameras? Why are you lashing out at me for some shit you caused? Every time a car passed by the house, he was turning the lights on and off, so if was the police, it would make them think we were not home. "Do you really think that is going to keep the police from coming up and knocking on the door? If it is them, they see the address outside, and you flicking the lights off right before they come up to the door is brilliant, right"? I went to bed with a splitting headache.

 The next morning, January 29, 2016, is when I saw the full extent of the damage to the car. I could not believe it. The entire right side of the car was dented up. We argued on the way to work as normal, in front of my daughter. He talked to me like I was a dude on the street and then followed it up with, "I don't care about you and that is why I can talk to you that way", all while he is swerving in and out of lanes. I got out of the car and said a prayer. "Lord, please let my daughter make it to school safely, unharmed and unhurt". When I made it into the office, I just simply said, "Good morning", and went to my desk. My coworkers knew something was wrong. One of my coworkers followed me downstairs and asked me what was wrong and I just let loose and started venting about everything. I was talking and crying so loud and hard, the security officer came over and asked was everything okay. My coworker simply replied, "Yes. She is just venting. She will be okay". Once I was done venting, I came upstairs to our office and sat at my desk, pulled out my phone and proceeded to tell him how wrong he was.

Then in true victim fashion, he started talking very foul and vulgar to me. "Don't, nobody want you with your dry pussy". But what he did not expect was the response back. "I will not take that from someone who all they want to do is bust a damn nut. I am done. It is over. I am moving me and my things out of the room and going into my daughter's room. My children and I are moving out. I cannot and will not do this with you anymore. I am unhappy and broke. This relationship is unhealthy and I refuse to be badgered, belittled, berated and de-womanized by you any longer. You can have all this mess. I do not care. I am DONE!" Later that night, I went and purchased an air mattress, amongst other things, and set up in my daughter's room until we moved. I removed all my things out of the bedroom and let him have it. "Janea, I am sorry. I will change. I promise. I love you so much". "No you will not. You will NEVER and I do mean NEVER change. It is all about you. All you do is eat, sleep, shit, smoke and want to fuck and I have been allowing you to do it. It stops right here and right now. I am DONE".

Chapter Nine

Seeing it Through Until the End

By the time we entered February 2016, things were strained and as I previously mentioned, I had already informed Lee that me and my children were moving out. I had stopped talking to him completely. Anytime he asked me a question, I would give one-word answers. Nothing less and nothing more as I had made my decision. The happiness was gone and in my eyes, it was never going to return because he was never going to change. The one thing that I did change was, I stopped listening to Lee and started to refocus my attention on God. I made a promise to God that if he opened the door for me just one more time, I was not going to walk through it, I would run through it. When I got the phone call on February 6, 2016, that I was approved for the place I inquired about, I was more than elated. I was ecstatic. I kept it a secret. Then, as luck would have it, he would lose his mind yet again.

Things started to take a terrifying turn. A week before Valentine's Day 2016, my uncle and I took my son to purchase his first vehicle in Avon, a suburb of Indianapolis, IN. Lee, of course, asked why was he not invited to go with us to purchase the car. I simply stated to him, "Because he (my son) does not want you to go and he asked for our uncle to take us". Oh, he was infuriated, to say the least and he felt left out of the entire process. But why should he have felt like he should have been included? It was over for us. Me and my children were buying our time and making the transition to move. The night before Valentine's Day, we had a huge argument. As I stormed away and headed to go and lay down in my daughter's room, he proceeded to grab my arm and punch a hole in the air mattress I purchased to get me to come in the room with him. He tried to make my daughter leave her room. "No, she is lying back down in her bed. She is not going into the room with your son. LET ME GO! EVERYTHING THAT I HAVE HAD, YOU HAVE

DESTROYED! GET YOUR DAMN HANDS OFF ME!" He looked at me in total astonishment, like he could not believe that I made that comment. He left the house for the night.

    The next morning was Valentine's Day. About a month or two before, he got a very playful, not trained, pit bull named Pebbles. Every time he would let her out, she ran through the entire house. He did not have any control over this dog. Well on Valentine's Day he was still mad and irate about what happened the night before and before my eyes could blink, he opened the door to that led from the garage to the house and let her run all throughout the entire house. And he knew this would make me mad because we basically had to close ourselves up in the room because she had no training. I was so mad and angry, that I began to cry, yell and scream. My son said, "Mom, let's go. We have another car now. Let's go. I will drive us. I don't care if there are not any tags on the car, let's go". And that is what we did. We went and got breakfast and I had to purchase another air mattress, but this time, I made him pay half of that money back. He should have paid for the entire air mattress considering he was the one who busted it, but I did not have time to argue with a man that I was not speaking to.

    As the week progressed, I began to make plans for our move. When I did tell my children that I found a place for us and that we were moving at the end of the month, they were very happy. "Mom, we get to have our own rooms back"? "Yes. You do". That was enough for them. On Wednesday, 2/17/16, I went to lie down as it was getting late and I was tired and had to get ready for work the next morning. It was around 11 PM and the phone rang. My sister was returning my phone call from earlier that day. As the phone was ringing, he was in the kitchen and he opened the door to my daughter's room because he heard the phone. "Who was that"? "What? Why does it matter? But since you must know, it was my sister returning my call". "Why is your sister calling you so late"? "Lee, good night. I don't feel like it with you tonight and I don't have time for your foolishness".

"Who was that man you were talking to on the phone"? "What? I was not talking to a man earlier this week. I was listening to a motivational video by Trent Shelton that I needed to hear for myself. Why does it matter? We are not together. We are moving out and moving on". "Janea, do you plan on us getting back to together"? "No, I do not". "Where are you all moving too"? "We are moving in with my uncle". Every time he asked where we were moving to, I always replied with that because I knew he would never show up to my uncle's house. "Janea, I have changed. Can't you see that"? "See what, if you love me, then let me go because I am not staying with you another damn minute. We are over. I have given you plenty of chances and you chose other things over this relationship and I am DONE".

On February 18, 2016, it was a just another day in the death trap house. We were both home from work and the kids were home from school. I was in my daughter's room like I had been for the past few weeks. He knocks on the door. "Janea, can I ask you a question". "What is it "? I replied. "I just want to know; how long have you been messing around and cheating on me? You were talking to some man the other night and then you said it was your sister calling, but you hung up with her too quick. So, I just want to know who it is". "Lee, I do not have time to listen to your shenanigans. Something is truly wrong with you". And that is how I ended the conversation. Did I expect that from him? Yes, I did. He had lost all power and control of the relationship. I was no longer the scared, intimidated person I used to be. I was the angry, pissed off black woman who had enough. The next morning would seal the coffin for us, but especially him.

Friday, February 19, 2016, would start like this. Lee came and knocked on my daughter's bedroom door. It was after six in the morning and the boys had left for school. Lee, who was as naked as a jaybird, absolutely no clothes on, knocks on my daughter's door. "Janea, can you come into the room for a minute"? "No, I am not coming into the room with you". I rolled back over and tried to go back to sleep. 20 or so minutes went past and another knock on the door, "Janea can you come in the room for a minute". I finally got up to go to use the bathroom. I stood at the entrance of the bedroom, "What do you want"? But I knew what he wanted and he was not getting it from me. "Come and lay down with me". "No. We have to get ready for work and she (my daughter) has to get ready for school". As soon as I turned my back to walk away from the bedroom entrance, he comes from behind me, literally picks me up, brings me into the bedroom, closes the door and would not let me out.

"How in the hell do I get us out this situation "? is what I am thinking to myself as he proceeds to sit me on his lap. "Let me go, Lee. I do not want to be in this room with you. Just let me go so we can get ready". "No, I am not going to let you go. What is wrong with you"? "Nothing is wrong with me. I do not want to sit on your lap. I want out of this room. We have to get ready to go". He continued not to let me go or out of his lap. "Okay, well let me sit in the chair". I went and sat in the chair and positioned myself closer to the window. He pulled me close to him. I pushed myself away one last final time, he completely snapped. He flew into a rage, just like he did exactly seven months prior to the date. "MAN, WHAT THE FUCK IS WRONG WITH YOU! YOU CHEATING ASS BITCH! YOU HAVE BEEN FUCKING ANOTHER MAN!" "NO, I HAVE NOT! LOOK AT US, WE ARE NOT HAPPY! I CANNOT DO THIS WITH YOU ANY LONGER! WE CANNOT DO THIS ANY LONGER!" We are both screaming at each.

My daughter came and knocked on the bedroom door, "Daddy, please stop yelling and screaming. You said that you would not scream and be mad like this anymore. You promised me. Please stop me". "I AIN'T YOUR DAMN DADDY. YOU MAMA HAS MADE DAMN SURE OF THAT. SHE BLOCKED ME FROM DOING ANYTHING FOR YOU. STOP CALLING ME DADDY! She walked away from the door and went back into her room. I went and sat back down in the chair still trying to figure out how I was going to get us out of there with him. He kept on screaming and hollering and before I knew it, he threw the entire chair with me sitting in it, on the floor. I quickly got up on my feet. He picked up the chair and threw the chair into the closet. It completely broke to pieces.

He took the remote-control holder to the television remotes and threw it into the closet as well. I broke apart as well. "YOU NASTY BITCH! DIDN'T YOU SAY YOU ALL WERE MOVING OUT?! GET ALL Y'ALL SHIT AND GET THE FUCK OUT RIGHT NOW!" As I started walking towards the door, he grabs me. "WHERE IN THE FUCK DO YOU THINK YOU ARE GOING"? "Didn't you just say you wanted me and my kids to leave? That is what you said right"? "BITCH, YOU AIN'T GOING NOWHERE!" Then just like you flip a switch, he starts crying, "What did I do? What did I do wrong? I love you. Please do not leave me". And then he comes and lays his head on my shoulder. I knew this would be the time to get out of the room.

I get to the edge of the bed and began to fake an asthma attack. I was able to open the door and get out of the room and go to the bathroom. By this time, my daughter emerged from her room. He proceeds to apologize to my daughter and then there was a knock at the door. He looked at me and asked, "Who called the police"? "How in the hell should I know. I have been locked in a room with you yelling and screaming for the past 15 minutes. Maybe one of the neighbors called". Then he turned to my daughter with rage, "Did you call the police"? She threw her hands up, "No, I promise I did not", while I stood in front of her thinking, "try it if you want to, I am going to get the bat, and your head will be the ball that will not be coming back!" "Janea, I am going to go back to jail. Just let them know we had a bad argument and make them leave".

As I answered the door, the officer asked me was he still there. "I just want him to leave", was my response to him. The first officer along with another officer came in. The officer asked, "Sir, do you have any weapons under the sheet"? Then, as a scared little boy, he replies, "No, I don't officer. I do not have any clothes on under here". We were separate by the police officers. Before the office began to question me, one of the first things he said to me was, "You are going to tell me everything that happened, because you did not just have the conversation I had with your daughter". It was her who called the police. I remembered, I left my cell phone in the room with her and she went into the back bedroom where no one could hear her and guided the officers to our house. He commended her for bravery and reassured her that Lee would no longer harm us ever again.

      I took Lee's son back to Nashville, TN on 2/21/2016 as Lee was returned to jail on 2/19/2016. Another no contact order was issued as all the logistics of what happened on that Friday began to be ironed out. The same process ensued as it did on 7/19/2015, the only exception, there was not a run to the emergency room. And this time, I followed through with every court date and every visit to the prosecutor's office to give a statement. As court dates were canceled more than once, we finally had a court date of September 6, 2016. About 4 days before our case, I met with the prosecutor and she informed me that my daughter may have to testify on the stand about her 911 call and I was also told that even though we would be in court, I would not be allowed in the courtroom while she was testifying against him.

      I did not know how to feel, let alone how she would feel about having to be in front of him yet again. All the counselors agreed to rearrange their schedules to be in court on that date just so she would recognize someone in the courtroom. I explained to her that she would have to go to court and talk to the court about the 911 call she made and she said, "Okay mommy. I am a big girl. I can do it". At the last minute, the prosecutor called and stated Lee accepted the plea agreement, and my daughter would not have to testify in court. And off to court, we went. I had not seen or heard from him since we went to court early in the year in March of 2016 to set the no contact order in place.

      The prosecutor presented our case to the judge. He was facing 6 years in prison. The judge read the charges off to him. She asked him was there anything he wanted to say to the court. He tried to turn around and apologize to me however, the judge put a stop to that. "Mr. Moore, no contact means no contact. Even though Ms. Page is in the courtroom, you are not to make any contact with her. All of your comments are to be directed to me". He proceeded to let the court know how sorry he claimed he was and how could he serve out any time he was given in Nashville, TN to be closer to his mother. He also showed her where he completed the Domestic Violence classes and Anger classes while he had been incarcerated.

She then asked me did I have any comments. "Your Honor, no one deserved to be treated the way myself, my children and his children were treated for that matter. He made life hell for everyone". He began to get upset. Then she spoke. "Mr. Moore, I understand wanting to return back to Nashville, TN and I am sure that would make Ms. Page happy, but you have to complete your time here. The sheer fact that a 9-year-old little girl had to call the police and save her life and the life of her mother is not right as you should have let her leave when she asked you to leave and you did not. You will be granted time served. You will be placed on GPS monitoring for 1 year and will be able to serve out your 2-year probation sentence in Nashville, TN provided they will accept you and provided you DO NOT violate the no contact order". Case closed. Well, I guess you know, he could not even do that correctly.

November 4, 2016, the day before my birthday, I received a phone call around 12:30 in the morning and guess who was on the other end of the phone. "Janea, just hear me out. I really am sorry. I wrote this letter to you while I was in jail and I want to read it to you. I am not sure how this works in Community Corrections and I am not sure when I will get out of here". "You have got to be kidding me. ARE YOU SERIOUS? You cannot honestly think that I want you back in my life or that I was coming to pick you up and you live with me and my kids again". That would have been a major setback for me. I listened to this letter that he wrote saying how much he needed me, wanted me back in his life, how he was sorry for what happened, oh, how beautiful I looked in court and how my daughter should not have had to go through what he put her through. "Are you done yet? I am DONE! This is over between us. I have nothing to say to you and why are you calling me"?

I hung up and he called right back. "Janea. I am sorry. I've changed. Just give me one more chance". "You changed what. You cannot even manage not to call me. And all the lies you told people about me when it was you the whole entire time. I AM DONE! I need for you to get it, understand it, know it and accept it. We are done. Stop calling me". Then he called on my birthday, 11/5/2016. "Janea, do you have time to talk"? "I do not understand why you cannot get this. We are DONE. It is OVER. Stop calling me". He called yet again on 11/7/2016. "Janea, can we talk"? "No, stop calling me", and I hung up. I was having lunch with my daughter that day. As soon as I made it out of the school and into my car, I called his mom and proceeded to ask her to have him stop calling me. I also explained to her that if he called me one more time, I was going to have him locked back up for violating the no contact order. I would not hear from him again until 1/9/2017.

	As I returned from my dental appointment on Monday, 1/9/17, the phone rang and showed a Carmel, IN phone number. I answered the call and it was him yet again and I snapped immediately. "Why in the fuck are you calling me! Stop calling me!", and hung up. Then about 20 minutes after him, the same mutual friend called begging me not to put him back in jail. I must admit, I thought about not returning him back to jail, but that thought quickly faded, as this was not about him or his feelings. This was about me and my children, our safety and well-being. Although I was victimized by him, I refused to be his victim any longer. I called his probation officer to report the violation of the order. I also filed a new police report regarding the violation of the order as well and he was returned to jail on 1/12/2017. He contested ever calling me on 1/9/17 when he was in court on 2/17/17, so I had to be present for the next court date and present documentation to prove he called me. I was mad as hell.

	Not because I had to go to court, but because my whole 2016 was spent going back and forth to the hearings and the prosecutor's office and I was tired of him playing the victim. We returned to court on 2/24/17 and this time, not only did I tell them about him calling me on 1/9/2017, I also told them about the 3 previous times he called.

      When it was all said, and done, he was sentenced to 3 years in prison, simply because he could not adhere to the orders given back on 9/6/2016. He felt like he was above the law, but the law quickly reminded him who was on top. Since the prison counts days as 2-for-1, his 3-year sentence is 1 ½ and he will be released on 10/31/2018. But the point is, that I stood up to him, fighting for my rights as a survivor and saw the process through to the end.

Chapter Ten

Finally, I Can Breathe

Finally, finally, finally, I can breathe. From 2011 to 2016, I felt like I had a choke hold on me or more like he was pressing his knee into my neck and I was not able to come up for air. I felt like the more I would try to free myself, the more he would knock me down. That was all over. My children and I are no longer subjected to any of the abuse he dished out to us. We have been able to put our lives back together piece-by-piece. Pieces of our lives were replaced with peace of mind, knowing he would never harm us again. I would take peace of mind over anything else because when you do not have peace of mind, you are not happy within. And in the final act of releasing him and having peace of mind and being able to exhale and breathe a little bit easier, I wrote this letter to him. This was me closing the door on a chapter of my life where the door should have never been reopened. This letter gives an account-by account detail of our relationship. This letter is dated on June 9, 2016, and reads as such:

"Dear Lee, As of June 9, 2016, I will end the chapter and close the book on a chapter of my life that should have never been re-opened. God closed that door for a reason, but I chose to open it, so I had to deal with the consequences that came with it.

My nightmare with you began on October 8, 2011. That is the day I drove to Tennessee for what I thought would be the new beginning with an old flame. I did not know much about what had transpired with you in the past, other than you were separated (not divorced) from your second wife. We had not seen each other for some 10 plus years. You didn't know much about how my life had changed either, except for the fact that I now had a daughter. In the

beginning, everything was cool, until the first argument we had in November of 2011. You were mad about me not giving you a key. The look in your eyes was one of rage, filled with hate. I could not believe what was going on, but that was the first sign of what was yet to come. I should have taken you back to TN then, but I chose to try to make it work as this was only one incident and because I did not want to be alone and I would much have had a piece of a man than not have one at all. But little did I know; this was just the beginning of what was yet to come.

There were arguments, on top of arguments and then there was the fateful day in late July, early August of 2012. The argument escalated to the first incident of domestic assault. I was snatched out of the locked car and pulled back into the house. I was thrown against the wall. You took my phone and threw it and it broke into pieces. You had me against the wall and I remember saying to you: "So now what? Are you going to hit me"? and you said: "I am not going to hit but I am going to show you what I am going to do to you". Then there was a knock at the door. Thankfully, it was the police and that was my exit. They asked me was I held against my will and instead of telling the truth that I was, because I feared what would happen, I told them no and could I get my daughter and leave. That was the first time my daughter had seen you in rare form and act a complete and total jerk and the first time she had seen her mother being treated like that but it was not the last.

The physical aspect of abuse stopped, but the mental, emotional and verbal abuse did not. From September of 2012 through December 30, 2013, there was not any physical abuse, but the mental, verbal and emotional abuse continued. Then on December 31, 2013, we had yet another heated argument while driving to take me to work and getting you some marijuana. I cannot remember exactly what we were arguing about, but I do remember while driving, I threw the car in park because I did not like how I was being treated and talked to. I remember you pulling over to a school on about 24th and Arlington and we were yelling and screaming at each other and I told you I would walk to work and you told me that if I continued to talk to you like that, you were going to hurt me. You yanked me by my collar and I remember fighting you *off. I remember, once we made it to our destination, we went at it again.*

I remember taking the engagement ring off and telling you that you could have it back. You then grabbed me by my collar, broke my necklace that was my grandmothers. You then proceeded to get out the car and knock on the door. You picked up the keys, but not the truck keys. I remember looking at myself and getting into the driver seat and praying the truck would not make that God-awful sound. When I turned the keys, and started the truck, you looked like OMG, don't leave me here. You knocked on the window and kept saying: "Janea, stop the car!" but I would not stop. All I could remember was trying to get away. Again, bruised and bloodied and I still had to go to work. You held on to the mirror and when I stopped the truck with force, you let go and I bagged out and kept driving. I went to the house to get my daughter and take her to our uncle's house. Again, I still went back to you and why I do not know. And again, no physical violence in 2014!

Your father passed on April 15, 2014, and then everything truly went to hell in a hand basket. You were so hurt and devastated by the loss of your father that instead of seeking help as your mother stated that you should have done, you continued to release verbal, mental and emotional abuse on all of us. You also began to dive deeper into smoking marijuana and drinking more. It was awful. Nothing seemed to go right. Then we go into a new year, 2015, and yet another violent outbreak.

I cannot recall the exact date in January, but it was January 2015. We had an argument that morning. You went to the shop and I went and got the oil changed in the truck. I came to get my items out of the car from the barber shop and you came outside, yet in a rage. You put your hand on my face and I knocked it out. We go into the barber shop, into the bathroom, and the arguing keeps going. We go back to the car. Trying to defend myself from you, you do not only bite me, but you smacked the ---- out of me also. At this point, I am

physically fighting with you, and manage to get out and run across the street screaming. I remember a guy coming and telling you the police were on the way and it was not worth it and you told him, "Man, stay out of it. This is my wife".

    I remember saying that I wasn't and running into the Dollar General store and again the police came and again you ran, like the coward you are. And yet again, I still came back to you. I remember one day in May of 2015, I was taking a bath and we were having an argument. You came in the bathroom and while I was in the tub, you proceeded to splash soapy water in my face, eyes and hair. We continued to argue and as I tried to put on my underwear, you continuously snatched them out of my hand and we began to throw things at each other. That happened often, then comes July 19, 2015.

    Arguing again from the previous night, I go to take Ryan to work and stop to get a coffee and tea like I would normally do on a Sunday morning. I come home and that is when everything went wrong. I now know, not only should I have let you leave, I should have let you go for good. The argument escalated and escalated. Then the physical violence began. Trying not to let you leave, I get in the car. Then I remembered the keys were left in the house. I went in to get them and you tried to leave and pushed me out the way. I pushed you back and when you pushed me again, you busted my lip. I went in the house and got the wrench and busted the window and that is when all hell broke loose. I have never been so violated and humiliated in all my life. I was snatched through a mesh, wire, steel door. You screamed at me that you hated me. You spit in my face, not once, not twice, but three maybe four times. You threw tea on me and then pushed me. I pushed you and then you pushed me again and this time, when I fell, my head hit a ceramic floor.

    With blood dripping down my face, I went to look at myself and begged for you to take me to the emergency room. We got in the car, and the arguing kept going. You called me a "Stupid Bitch", continued to tell me how much you hated me and spit on me yet again. I then smacked you in the face. You then decided that you would not take me to the emergency room, but instead back to the house. We were on the bridge going over to 25th and Post Rd and you back handed me in my mouth and took my keys. Now bleeding again, I am begging for my keys and you are telling me no you would not give them to me. We made it back to the house and I was walking around the house and looking for my daughter so I could drive myself to the ER and you came in behind me saying, "Why are you calling her name. She is not here".

Then you said to me, "I hate you". I said, "I hate you". I turned my back to walk away and you pulled me by my hair, pinched and twisted the skin on my right arm and turned me around. As I am trying to kick you off me, you grabbed my right leg and pulled it all the way up to my head until it popped and I screamed. You then carried me to the couch and sat me on your lap and that is when you began to realize how serious it was. I got up off your lap and went into the bedroom to assess myself and said to myself, "What are you doing? He is going to kill you". I got my keys and not knowing where my daughter was, drove myself to the hospital.

I allowed myself to let you make me not only feel guilty about you spending 24 days in jail, but I also let you take my self-esteem away and made me feel like I was nothing. I was at my lowest of low. But to understand my state of mind and why I continued to go back to you, you must first realize that I was truly a victim of domestic violence, however, in your eyes, it was never that. It was always my fault that this happened, and I truly began to believe that. Still thinking things would work, moved yet into another house with you, but this time, I was slowly coming back to myself and regaining the power and control you had over me, through the help of counseling I had been receiving and continue to receive to this day.

The mental, emotional and verbal abuse continued. I was learning how to stand up to you and gain my fighting power back. I was no longer happy. I had truly hit rock bottom with you. I had allowed you to suck all the life and energy out of me. I knew once I had hit rock bottom, the only way was to slowly and surely work my way out and up. My son had voiced on numerous occasions that he was going to kill you if I and his sister were ever hurt by you again. I knew then that it was time to leave, because I was not going to allow my son to ruin his future because you wanted to be a coward, not a man, but a coward. I moved out of the room on January 28, 2016.

However, to keep the peace, I continued to do things that I know I should not have done and as a woman and an adult, I can admit that I was wrong. I then finally realized, this was making me feel worse about myself as all you wanted to do was have sex and bust a nut and I finally said, "I can no longer do this. I do not care how much you want sex, get it from someone else". I had given all I could give until I could no longer give because I truly had nothing left to give. All I could do was start working on a plan for getting me and my children out of harm's way. During this time, I was making arrangements on finding a place and keeping us safe until we moved at the end of February 2016; that all came to a head-on February 19, 2016.

While you were making me out to be the bad person, it was you doing wrong. It was you using and wallowing in drugs and alcohol. It was you that lost control and when you began to lose power and control over me, you did not know how to handle it. You single handedly dismantled what was supposed to be a family. But the change also began when I started to become emotionally, physically and mentally detached from you and that, Mr. Lee L. Moore, Sr., you could not handle. I would no longer allow myself to talk to you while you were smoking. And you were mad because you I would not talk to you when you wanted me to, but by this time, I was tired and did not want to talk anymore. I just wanted to leave. Get my babies and go. You were always used to leaving women high and dry, but never a woman leaving you high and dry. WELL, THIS WOMEN DID!!!! You see, I so thank you for showing me how I should not be treated because it has opened the door for a new man to love me and treat me like the QUEEN that I am. I thank you so much for doing wrong because it has opened the door for things to be done right and for me to be treated with RESPECT.

I am so grateful for all the times you told me that and I quote, "Ain't no man going to put up with you trying to dictate to them and trying to run a relationship", because it has opened the door for a new man to show me that I do not have to do it by myself or go at it alone. I am so grateful for your not trusting me because it has opened the door for a new man to TRUST me with his heart. And finally, I am so grateful for you not loving me unconditionally because a new man will LOVE me unconditionally, flaws and all. I am not just someone he wants to "screw", I am truly someone HE WILL WANT TO LOVE. You see, there is a man that is out there that WILL TRULY LOVE ME and that is what you were scared of because one man's trash (which is what you considered me because every time you called me a BITCH, you were truly calling me TRASH) is truly, truly another man's TREASURE.

You see, I personally do not care about how much time you did back in July/August of 2015 or how much time you are given now because the fact remains on July 19, 2015, when my head hit the ceramic floor, I could have died. Instead, I walked away with 10 stitches (6 behind my left ear and 4 over my left eye), bruises up one side of my body and down the other, busted lip in different places. That was physical. I also am now dealing with an optic nerve issue with my right eye, that has been caused by this incident as well along with trying to recover from your smoking cigarettes and marijuana around me and knowing I was suffering from asthma. On February 19, 2016, when you flipped me out of the chair and continued to flip out, I could have died.

I thank God daily that I did not. I see stories where women have not made it out of domestic violence situations and leaving children and families behind to ask the questions, "Why"? You see, I realize that I was truly a victim of this vicious cycle of Domestic Violence. Looking back, all the signs were there, I just chose not to look that deep into it because I always said, "This would never be me or my life", but it was my life for 5 years. I do not care about how much time you are given. You will never be able to do this to another woman again in life and if you do, then you are the fool. There is nothing you can say to me that would make me feel any different than what I am feeling today and from here on out.

It has now been almost 4 months since this last incident has happened and almost a year since the 1st incident has taken place. My financial status is getting back on track and my children are happy and most importantly, I am happy. I have PEACE IN MY LIFE. PEACE OF MIND. I AM FINALLY ABLE TO BREATHE. You no longer have power or control over me. And this may sound crazy to most, but for me, it is not. I forgive you for all the wrong doing you have done to me. I forgive you because, for me to move on to the next chapter of my life, I must have freedom of this chapter and remove all power and control away from you.

I must have closure for not only myself, but my children, and my family and this, my friend, Mr. Lee Moore, Sr., is truly closure at its best. I also forgive you because I am no longer your victim, I and my children are the VICTORS in all of this because we are no longer in your grasps of the mental, physical, verbal and emotional abuse you have dished out to us. You do not WIN. WE are no longer your charity, victimless, basket cases we once used to be. I do not harbor any ill will against you for what you have done to me and my children.

I leave you with the below scriptures from James 4:2-3, 8-10

"You want what you don't have, so you scheme and kill to get it. You are jealous for what others have and you can't possess it, so you fight and quarrel to take it away from them. And yet the reason you don't have what you want is you don't ask God for it. And even when you do ask, you don't get it because your whole motive is wrong-you want only what gives you pleasure".

"Draw close to God, and God will draw close to you. Wash your hands, you sinners, and purify your hearts you hypocrites. Let there be tears for the wrong things you have done. Let there be sorrow and deep grief. Let there be sadness instead of laughter and gloom instead of joy. When you bow down and admit your dependence on him, he will lift you up and give you honor.

Janea Page"
And this was the day I could release, relax and let go and let God continue to help me work on me. Yes, I did have days where I wanted to scream, but instead of screaming, I would just BREATHE. And sometimes just stepping back and taking deep breaths and talking to GOD is all the strength I needed to make it through the day.

Chapter Eleven

Moving ONE STEP FORWARD

There you have it. After all the pain and drama in my life over the past 5 years, I am finally able to move ONE STEP FORWARD, one day at a time. It has taken a lot to get to the point in my life where I am at today. I am a totally different person than what I was 5 years ago. What have I done differently today than what I did in the past? Plain and simple, I stopped listening to the man and started listening to GOD. God is the only reason why I am where I am today. Without His guidance and help, I would still be in the same position I was in 5 years ago. This was a challenge not because of God and His guidance, but because of me and not willing to submit to His plan for my life. Once I submitted to His plan of action, everything started to fall into place. Here are some of the things that I did differently than I would have done in the past.

Put God First

When you stop putting God first and put man first, you are headed down a path of destruction. And that is exactly what happened. I put a man in front of what God was saying to me. I often say it like this. This was like a 3-lane highway for me. Lee was in the lane to the left; God was in the middle lane and I was in a lane on the right. God is insisting that I come down the middle lane. However, I am fighting God and I go down my lane, because to me, the outcome of happiness is at the end of my lane. God quickly showed me how wrong I was. So then, instead of turning around and going down God's lane, I came up Lee's lane, the wrong way heading in the wrong direction. What I saw as a future with Lee was nothing more than despair, mishaps, and misfortune at the end of his lane.

God kept showing me what was at the end of both the right and left lanes that I had made a choice to go down. I could hear Him saying to me, "If you continue to go down either one of those paths, you will not make it out". I should have taken God serious on 7/19/2015, but I did not. I choose to take Lee's path, where I was headed the wrong way altogether. That path was one filled with guilt, shame, and despair. It was a dark and lonely road because I chose it. God had to let me continue down that road so He could show me what was at the end of it. I finally chose God's path in January of 2016 and have not looked back since.

To have peace of mind, body, and soul, you must listen to God. He will never leave you or forsake you. I can remember writing in my journal one day as I was starting down His path, "God never lost sight of me and my children. Please keep us close to you, out of harm's way". Once I tuned anyone, everyone, and everything out, I could hear God speaking to me. His words were ever so clear to me. I also made a promise to Him that whatever door He opened for me this time, I was running through it and that is what I did. We must take God at his word. We must learn to trust Him, lean on Him, and depend on Him. God has never said it was going to be easy. If done right and His way, not man's way, He will supply you with all your needs to make it out of any situation. He closes doors for a reason. And once those doors are closed, they should stay closed, never to be re-opened. You will know when God has a new door opened for you because it will be specifically for you and absolutely no one can take that away from you when God gives it to you. You must take His path and His words serious, and LISTEN. He is the teacher. We are the students. One of the best scriptures that helped me through this difficult time was Philippians 4:13 which reads, *"I can do all things through Christ which strengthens me"*. This made me realize that I can do this. It may not be easy, but no matter what, I can do the right thing, get out of this horrible relationship, and start over fresh and new. You must also have Faith as well. Faith makes everything possible. Consider another verse in the bible. Matthew 17:20 reads, *"You didn't have enough faith,"* Jesus told

them. "I assure you, even if you had faith as small as a mustard seed, you could say to this mountain, 'Move from here to here,' and it would move. Nothing would be impossible".

Stop making excuses.

In moving ONE STEP FORWARD, it meant I had to stop making excuses for myself and start accepting and being held accountable for my actions in what had been done. I had to take a long, hard look at myself in the mirror and come face-to-face with the person who was staring back at me. In looking at myself, I saw a person who was worn down and worn out. I made excuses or had quick comebacks for anything and everything. I can remember I went to work one day and I had a huge bruise on my arm from fighting with Lee and one of my co-workers saw it and asked me what happened, and the first thing I did was making an excuse as to what happened instead of being truthful about it and possibly getting some much-needed help at that time. As I began to look at myself whole-heartedly, the biggest excuse I had, was, "I am his victim and I will not be able to get out of this mess". I had not accepted what happened to me nor did I hold myself accountable for my actions.

For me to stop making excuses about being a victim of DV, I had to let go of the stigma that goes along with being a victim of DV. I had to let go of thinking that I was a victim. I had to see myself in a different light. As I began to accept being a victim of abuse, my negative excuse went to one of positivity and I saw it as, "Although, I am victim of having a domestic violent act committed against me, I refuse to be a victim of domestic violence circumstances. This act of violence committed against me was not my fault and I refuse to accept it as my own. I am truly a VICTOR and SURVIVOR", and I knew this is how God saw me as well. I had to make myself accountable for allowing this man to commit these horrible acts against me as well. I had countless times to leave him, but I chose to stay. That was the biggest mistake I made and falling for someone who was narcissistic in nature, who consistently showed his true colors daily and displayed a Dr. Jekyll Mr. Hyde personality to others.

An excuse is a glorified lie we must keep going. Once we make one excuse we must keep making excuses to cover up whatever is going on in our lives. When excuses are being made the only person or persons we are hurting is ourselves or others around us whom we love and care about. Instead of facing the truth, we would much rather make an excuse as to what happened and why it happened. One cannot absolutely move forward by making excuses about the past and present because it will hinder the outcome of your future. Stop making excuses as to why you need a significant other in your life. Having a significant other is not a need, it is a want. We don't WANT to be alone, although some of us NEED to be alone. We need to be alone because we NEED to be able to hear God's words and what he is trying to minister to us in our time of need.

Also, we need to stop making excuses for someone who absolutely does not give a damn about what happens to you. All they care about is how we are going to fix their problems and they cannot even help us fix our own problems and they are not worried about it either. Don't get so caught up on handling someone else's issues. Joel Olsteen has stated in a previous sermon, "We should all have hours of operations when we should handle other people's problems. We find ourselves making excuses and trying to fix everyone else's problems that we have little time to focus on our own issues". My hours of operation sign say "CLOSED". We cannot get wrapped up or focused on others excuses as to why they are in the situation they are in. We must focus on not making excuses for ourselves and push forward to the next step.

<u>Committed to me, myself and I</u>

What do I mean by this? I was so used to ending a relationship just to jump right back into a new relationship with someone I barely knew or had any interest in. If they were interested in me, then I went along for the ride. I put them and their needs before myself and my own needs always and I am woman enough to admit it. I did not value myself, or my self-worth. My self-worth was placed on the back-burner. All I knew was, I did not want to be alone. I was used to having a warm body next to me. But what did that do in return, absolutely nothing but add hurt, headaches, heartaches, and heartbreaks. I never took the time out to LEARN about the person I was about to get into a relationship with. Nothing was meaningful. We were never friends, but friendly with each other, if you know what I mean. But I can guarantee this, if I knew half of the information that I know today, I would not have been in any of the relationships I was in. The biggest blessing in two of my failed relationships are my children and the best blessing of this last relationship was getting out with my life.

Today, I am perfectly fine with being alone. I do not need a relationship to make me happy. I have learned to be happy on my own and by myself and I am okay with that. I needed time to heal from all the past hurts and wounds from the failed relationships. I had to learn how to LOVE and RESPECT myself all over again, and that is okay. I had to put my self-worth and VALUE before anyone else's. I also had to learn that my needs and the needs of my children come before that of any man and his needs. We come first. Sometimes, it takes for you to hit rock bottom, to recognize what you mean to you, not anyone else, but to YOU! Sometimes it is at our lowest points in life, we learn to love ourselves, put our self-worth and respect before others and stop allowing ourselves to being treated like we are doormats, basically being stepped/walked all over by others. It is also at this very point that we hear God more clearly than we have before. We must be willing to listen to get back to loving ourselves and sometimes we may not agree with the path He is taking us down, but God does not make any mistakes. At the end of the day, He knows what is best for us and he will not steer us wrong.

Create an Exit Plan

When I had finally had enough, I started working on how I could remove me and my children away from the toxic and unhealthy place we were at the time. I became quiet, started listening to God and working on exit plan on getting us out of there. It was not easy. I could not search for homes in his presence and I had to be very secretive in how I planned things. I could only let key people know who I could trust about what my plans were. Anytime he asked me about our whereabouts as to where we were moving to, I would state to him, "We are moving in with my uncle", because I knew this was the one place he would not show up to. I also let one coworker that I trusted know and my direct supervisor know as well.

The reason being, they knew my routine and if something happened outside the scope of my routine, then they would know something went wrong. I made sure that all business conducted was completed during work hours. Yes, I am aware when we are working, we should be working, however, in this circumstance, it is imperative that your employer/immediate supervisor is aware of your situation and why this business cannot be conducted in the privacy of your own home. Right now, your place of employment is your privacy location and can be treated as such during this difficult transitional period.

Create a safety exit plan that best suits the needs of you and your children. You should have more than one location that is considered a "safe place". Keep a journal in a safe, secure place away from your home, where your abuser cannot retrieve it and read it. This is key, because if the abuser finds this information, things can take a drastic turn for the worse. I have heard of too many horror stories where women, in general, were trying to leave an abusive situation, returned to retrieve their items, only to be killed. I kept a journal locked away in my desk.

I let my co-workers know it was there as it held key detailed information just in case something went horribly wrong during this extremely delicate, yet dangerous time. You must remember, you are fighting for your life and the lives of your children if you have them, so things must be done in secrecy. There are several different sites and resources that are available via the internet that have "Personalized Safety Plan" templates that can be printed and used to help execute your plan. One website that offers various and helpful information is www.dvrc-or.org. This stands for Domestic Violence Resource Center. It addresses all forms of domestic violence committed towards women, men and children.

Conduct business away from home and preferably not on a cell phone. Most abusers are accusers in nature. One way they try to monitor your activity is through cell phone usage. And the cell phones of today are not like the ancient ones in the past. Our cell phones, or rather, smart phones are computers and anything and everything can be tracked. Most abusers think you should not have any privacy and therefore your cell phone to them is not yours nor is it private and they feel they should be able to look at it at any time. This gives them a chance to go through and read emails, text messages, question you about different contacts within your phone they do not know about. Why, you ask?

It is because they are insecure with themselves. It has nothing to do with you. They have a level of insecurity they have yet to address and so to take the heat off them, they start to blame you. If the only way you can conduct business is through your cell phone, then make sure your phone is locked and the only way to access it would be to put in a numeric code that only you will know. When turn your phone off and back on, make sure the first screen that comes up is a secure keypad screen where you must place your passcode to use the phone.

Execute the Exit Plan

Now that the safety exit plan had been created, it was time to execute it. The hardest part was determining when it would be a good time to move and how safe would it be. Although he knew we were moving, he did not know where and I did not want him to know either. This is the
reason we ended up living with each other back after the incident in 2012. So, how was this
going to be pulled off? Yeah, there was only one car, which belonged to me, but I would have to
fight just to get my own keys from him sometimes because of all the damn questions he
would ask. So, in my mind, I figured, if I dropped him off at the shop, he could not get back to
the house quickly.

He would have to call me to come and pick him up. But the downfall was
and risk would be, he would probably have some else bring him. And moving in the middle of
the night was too risky and noisy. But no matter the risk, we were out of there. We had a place
to go, and no one outside of my uncle and co-worker knew where it was. I went ahead and
reserved the moving truck. And as luck would have it, when we had the last altercation on
2/19/2016, he got sent back to jail, and the safety exit plan went off without any problems on
Saturday, 2/27/2016.

I was prepared to leave him with nothing but ourselves, and completely start over, from clothing, furniture and appliances. I was prepared, because material items can be replaced.

Your lives cannot be replaced. Stick to the plan you have created and if this means you all must
leave without nothing, then do it. There are various organizations that will help you to replace
what you left. Your focus is having safety away from a violent person. Also, put a "NO
CONTACT" order on file with your local law enforcement office. This is for the purposes of
if your accuser happens to find out your whereabouts, he will be immediately be picked up and
jailed and charged with INVASION OF PRIVACY OR VIOLATION OF A VALID NO CONTACT ORDER. This does work. As mentioned in a previous chapter, Lee contacted me 4 times. He is now in prison, all because he violated the no contact order.

Chapter Twelve

Self Help Guide to Continuing Moving ONE STEP Forward

Once I was removed from the toxic, unhealthy relationship I had been in, there were still several steps I had to take to continue to move ONE STEP FORWARD. This is for anyone who is battling to remove themselves from any unhealthy relationship, struggling to love themselves and trying to gain a better understanding of why this happened to them.

1. **Face your fears.**
   In continuing with moving forward and rebuilding a new and improved you, begin to face your fears. One of the biggest fears I had was being alone. Being alone is what was needed. Face this fear head-on. We all hate to be rejected. We feel that if someone rejects us, they do not have any interest and while this may be true, being rejected is not a bad thing. For some of us, it is needed. This may be the way God may be keeping a door closed that we are trying to open and we do not know what's on the other side. Although scary, because some of us have never been alone a day in our lives, alone is what we need to be. We need to be able to face the nights alone, knowing that the only comforter we have now is God and He is all the person we need. Basically, in a nutshell, we need to face the fear of loneliness.

   We must also learn how to stay out of our own way. Sometimes, we block ourselves and our blessings because we are scared to face what is on the other side of the door. However, this is where walking by faith and not by sight comes in. (2 Corinthians 5:7). God can do all things but fail and you must know that as you are walking out on faith, He has your back. You may not like the path He is leading you down and that is okay, but God does not make any mistakes. He is leading you down this path for a reason and it is to make you a better you. To show you that life can be so much better if you put your trust in Him and not in man. Some of us would rather listen to a person who has nothing going for themselves and cannot keep a handle on their own life, but they do not have a problem with telling someone else how to live their life. My purpose is not to tell anyone how to live their life, my purpose is showing others there is a better way to live your life.

2. **Seek Outside Help.**
We all need someone to talk with or to talk about issues we are facing in life, especially after we have gone through traumatizing experiences of being abused. However, some of us are scared to talk with anyone because we are scared we are going to be judged by them; we may receive unhealthy advice from others and we may be scared to hear the truth about ourselves. We do not want to hear anyone tell us anything about what we have done wrong. We do not want to be held accountable for any of those actions or how many times we have gone to a family member or friend about an experience with our significant other that has put our life and the lives around you in jeopardy. Being afraid their response to us will be, "Don't leave, you need to stay and work it out with him/her for the sake of your family".

I have an even better example. Back in the spring of either 2014 or 2015, following my abuser, I joined a new church in the city where we lived, under a new pastor. I had a one-on-one conversation with the pastor with concerns that I had about the then relationship I was in with the person who abused me. The pastor went and told my abuser everything we talked about. You could only imagine the look on my face when he came back and told me everything I had discussed in what I thought was private with the pastor. Not only did I feel betrayed by pastor, I felt like he had broken my trust, and I never looked at the pastor the same.

It was at this point, my abuser made me feel so guilty and I felt like I did not have anyone to confide in. So, I am not advising anyone not to listen to family, close friends or clergy for that matter. What I am saying is listen carefully to the advice given. If your family, friend, or clergy members/staff know you are being abused and they advise you stay in an unhealthy relationship with anyone, then you need to consider not seeking any more advice from them. They are more of a hindrance than help. Listening to the wrong advice is not only the wrong thing to do, it is detrimental and life threatening. Too many women, men and children have lost their lives due to bad advice from others.

Seeking outside help from a counselor or counseling agency, is one of the best resources around. Counselors are trained to deal with various types of situations. They have a way of making you see what others have done, they also make you see what you are doing wrong (which is why, again, some of us are scared to go to counseling). Counseling has a way of making you hold yourself accountable for your actions or for what you have allowed to happen in an unhealthy relationship. It was through counseling that I learned I feared being by myself, rather a fear of being lonely, because I never dealt with the issues from past relationships. I continuously jumped from one relationship to the next and did not allow myself time to heal from the hurt and the pain of the previous relationship.

My family and close friends would tell me that I needed time to heal, but I felt like they did not want me to be in a relationship. It wasn't until I sat down with my counselor and told her my story. As we dove deeper into my past, she showed me the pattern of how I jumped from relationship to relationship with no down time in between. This is a person whom I had never met before until 8/2015. She knew nothing about me but could show me things about me that I did not want to see nor that I wanted to hear. She sent me home with questions to answer so we could discuss during our next session to help better understand why I followed the same pattern.

If it is to the point where you absolutely must leave with urgency, as it is a matter between life and death, let your counselor or counseling agency know immediately. They can work with the local authorities to help place you in emergency housing for the safety of not only you, but for your children as well and due to the Health Insurance Portability and Accountability Act (HIPAA) regulations, your counselor is not allowed to give out any Personal History Information (PHI) regarding your where-abouts. This is a federal act. Your life may depend on it.

3. **Obtain a No-Contact Order.**

If you have not done so prior to you leaving your abuser, make sure you complete a no contact order. This is for your protection and safety. List all addresses you think your abuser may show up to. You can list your children's school, work address, relative's address. In my case, I listed the barber shop he used to work at as well, because it was less than a mile away from the school my daughter attended. In most states, if someone has been involved in a domestic violent disturbance and the perpetrator is jailed, a NO CONTACT order is automatically given by the judge, but you also must go to your local precinct and complete a NO-CONTACT order immediately; if he/she violates the NO-CONTACT order, a warrant will be placed for their arrest immediately. And I know the first thing that someone will say is, "This does not work". But I am here to let you know that it does. If you think your abuser will try to contact you, here are steps you should consider:

a. **Change your phone number.**
Change your number and ONLY GIVE IT THOSE YOU TRUST and WILL NOT BETRAY YOU. I know you are probably thinking, "I should be able to give it to anyone in my circle". Wrong. The main goal of an abuser is to seek and destroy. Remember, they are like chameleons. They portray themselves to look one way in front of friends and another way behind closed doors. They prey on making others feel guilty as well. They may say, "I love her so much and I need to speak with her" or "She has my children. I just need to make sure they are all okay". This is a trap. Make sure the local authorities have your new number, along with a family member you trust. Also, make sure your direct supervisor has it and if you keep a journal at work, that would be a great place to store it also. Again, I would not give it to mutual friends, because they may not always have your best interest at heart. This is about the safety of you and your children.

b. **Join the Address Confidentiality Program (ACP).**
This is also another safety measure. Remember, local addresses are public information and can be looked up via the internet, if you have chosen not to make

your address private. This program allows you to set up a PO Box that is registered with the Attorney General's Office. This post office box can only be used for official business and public record information. For more information concerning how to apply for a confidential post office box in your area, visit the following website: http://victimsofcrime.org, Stalking Resource Center, a resource of the National Center for Victims of Crime. You should also contact your local authorities in your area or you should contact your local Attorney General's office.

c. **Log all Phone Calls.**
If you decide not to change your phone number or you change your phone number and your abuser somehow gets a hold of it, keep a log of each time he/she has called you and contact the authorities immediately. My abuser contacted me from a different phone number. I listed the numbers in my phone as "DO NOT ANSWER", so if he called, I would know not to answer, but to also be able to show the officer, this was the number he called from. Pull your cell phone records because this will be needed to prove your case if you should have to return to court for them violating the NO CONTACT set in place. If you are not able to pull your cell phone records, try to do a screen shot of your phone log and email it to yourself or list it in the journal you keep in a safe place. In the event, something happens, the authorities will be able to use your journal as a tracking log of each time he/she has contacted you.

4. **Gain Control of Your Life.**
Survivors of domestic violence often find their lives have been torn apart by not only their abusers, but others who are

close to them as well. Not only are you dealing with the shame of being abused, for some, they are dealing with the constant judgement of others. I have been saying, "I will no longer give pieces of me to anyone who cannot bring peace to me". In other words, let go of anyone who does not mean you any good. You are in control of your life. No one else but you. You are an adult and you make your own decisions. Stop letting others who have little interest in your life have so much say as to what goes on in it. Also, don't make yourself readily available to other people to lay their problems on you. Before long, you will find yourself trying to solve your problems and theirs too. They will have gone on about their business and you are still trying to work out their issues. I am still trying to get my life and the lives of my children back on track and you should too. Get rid of all the clutter within your life. You have removed the abuser, now it is time to remove the people who you have allowed to keep you in a dark, unhappy place because they are unhappy and miserable themselves.

5. **Believe in Yourself.**
Outside of your children and God, only one person believes in you and that is YOU. You must believe that you have the strength and courage to leave and stand up to the person who abused you. Don't let fear stop you from fighting for yourself, standing up for your rights, and seeing it through until the end. P.U.S.H. your way through if you have to. If you don't believe in you, then who else will. Have the courage to step forward and let others know that you were a victim, but now you are a SURVIVOR and if you have survived this, then let the world know you can survive anything. If no one else believes in you, I believe in you. I believe that you will be able to pull through this traumatic

experience and come out shining bright like the diamond I know you are.

6. **Remove, Rebuild, Restore.**
For most women, men, and children, their abusers have kept them alienated from family and friends. For the most part, an abuser has control of every aspect of their victim's life. They control who they see and who they talk to. Now that you are no longer under their control, it is time to do the three R's: **Remove**, **Rebuild** and **Restore**.
   a. Remove all the toxic, negative, and unhappy people out of your life. They are in a negative place, and if they had their way you would be right at the bottom with them. Let them go and move on with life. You will find that while you are continuing to move up, they are stuck in the same place, complaining about the same thing, which is absolutely nothing.
   b. Now that you have removed all the negative people out of your life, it is time to rebuild yourself. You have been under the control of someone else who has controlled every aspect of your life, from what you could wear to what you could spend. It is time for you to rebuild yourself and figure out what it is that you love about yourself. Take the time to build your self-esteem back up. Build it back by not listening to what others have to say or how they feel about you. Look in the mirror and look at the person staring back at you. Let that person know you love them without a shadow of doubt and let them no one can or will hurt you. You are saying this to yourself because you are staring back at yourself in the mirror.
   c. Start to restore past relationships with close friends and family members that were once lost and broken. Don't rush the process as you will have plenty of time to catch up with them. Try to limit the conversation

on the abuse you have endured. Rather, focus on how you can start to allow your family to become an intricate part of your life again. Nothing will be like it was in the past, yet this experience should bring you all closer and make the bond between you and your family stronger. It should also remind you, not to allow anyone to keep you away from your family. For some, family is all you have.

7. **Build Financial Ground.**
Now that you are on the track to getting your life back in order, you should start working on a plan to get your finances in order. Most women and men who emerge from a domestic assault, come out broke, without one dime and no one to help them financially. There is no money left for anything because he/she has taken every dime. Start to gain financial ground by doing the following:
   a. **Create a budget**. There are several templates that can be found on the internet to help you create a realistic budget.
   b. **Live within your means**. You cannot live like the Joneses. Do things and buy the things you know are within your means and that you can afford. Don't spend your last penny on anything that is a want and not a necessity. Remember, you are building financial stability.
   c. **Pay your bills on time**. Paying bills late can cause issues. If not careful, you will find yourself trying to pay the past-due and current bill at the same time. Most people are either paid every two weeks or semi-monthly. Set up your bills, according to how you are paid. For instance, we all know our rent or mortgage is due on the 1st of every month. So, this should come out of the first paycheck and so forth and so on. For

some, it will be the last paycheck. However, your pay days fall, set your bills up to be paid in the manner as well.

    d. **Start a savings challenge.** One of the goals I have set for myself and my children was a savings challenge, called the 52 Week Savings Challenge. How money is saved is, for every week in the year, you save $1 and every week increases by a dollar so by the time the end of the year has come, you would have saved $1378. There are several different templates on the internet for this challenge as well. Challenge yourself to save this money instead of wasting money on items you don't need.

8. **Start goal digging.**
Set realistic goals for yourself that you would like to accomplish. Write them down in a table or type them up on the computer. The goal can be anything you think of that you want to accomplish. As you began to accomplish and complete the goal, mark it off the list and move on to the next one. Some of them may be short term goals while others will be long-term. That's okay. It does not matter how long you take to complete them as these are your goals and you are not in a rush to complete them. You have all the time in the world.

As I bring this chapter of my life to a close, I want people to remember this. I am a mother, daughter, sister, aunt and a niece, but above all, I am a SURVIVOR of a vicious cycle of abuse that many women, men, and children battle with daily and many do not survive. Domestic violence did not defeat me, nor did it stop me. It helped me to realize, my strength comes from God, and He gave me the strength and power to defeat it, moving ONE STEP FORWARD, one step at a time

Resources

Piecing your life back together after domestic violence can be difficult. We all need people and places to turn to for assistance, advice, or just a listening ear. It could be anything from counseling to financial advice. Here are a few resources you can consider to help put your life back together, piece by piece.

Counseling Services

- There are several different counseling centers in the Indianapolis, IN area. One specifically works with women, men and children who have been affected by various types of acts of violence that have been committed against them. **The Legacy House** services are free of charge. For more information regarding their services, contact The Legacy House. Visit them at: The Legacy House, 2505 N. Arlington Ave., Indianapolis, IN 46218. Phone: 317-554-5272. Facebook: @LegacyHouseIndianapolis.

Support Group

- There are not many support groups where men, women, young adults and children can share their stories, use their voice and relate to others who have been through the same traumatic experience they have been through. ONE STEP FORWARD, is a support group that was created by me, Janea Adrian Page. The group was created to help others who have been through the same or similar experience as I have, empower and help navigate life after abuse. Additional information on ONE STEP FORWARD can be found at: www.onestepforwardmmxvi.webs.com and via at Facebook: @ONESTEPForwardMMXVI. We can also be reached by email at onestepforwardmmxvi@gmail.com.

Financial Services
- As I began to navigate life after domestic violence, I had to put my finances back in order. My finances suffered a lot because I was taking care of 6 people on basically one income. Today, with the help of others, I am gaining back financial freedom. What worked best for me was to file bankruptcy, a Chapter 13. I am repaying debt that I owe, through a payment plan set up by the US Bankruptcy Court. If filing bankruptcy is an option for you, outside of Chapter 13, you may want to consider wanting to file a Chapter 7, which wipes all your debt clean, except for student loans. However, once you have filed a Chapter 7, you are not allowed to file Chapter 7 for 8-10 years.

- While some may be able to hire an attorney to assist with cleaning up their financial mess, others may not. If you are not able to afford a bankruptcy attorney, you may want to consider obtaining a financial planner. Depending on what services you may need, financial planners are great resource for assisting with creating a budget and can teach you how to reduce the amount of debt you may currently have. Financial planner, Cynthia Newman, is one of those great resources. She, along with her husband, are partners with Primerica Financial Services. They provide a long list of financial services from preparing a financial plan, creating a realistic financial budget, to investment services and life insurance policies. For additional information regarding their services, she can be reached by email at cynthianewman@primerica.com.

- Another avenue to consider when it comes to trying to find financial stability and financial peace, would be to invest in credit repair services. Here is how credit repair services work. A monthly fee is paid to the credit repair service of your choice. Fee amounts do vary depending on the company. The company pulls a copy of your complete credit file. Once the derogatory items are identified, the credit repair service (CRS) will dispute the derogatory items to all three credit bureaus: TransUnion, Equifax and Experian. All have 30 days to respond to the dispute filed. If the company fails to respond or dispute the charge, it is removed from your credit file. There are several reputable companies throughout the United States. One credit repair company, **Social Coaching**, is a consulting agency which helps those who need "credit repair". Founded by Robin Sobomehin, the company prides itself on efficient and effective credit repair tactics to remove those negative items from your credit report, which in turn, helps to increase your credit score. Additional information on pricing and how to begin the program can be found on Facebook: Social Coaching, @MyCreditCoach. Let them turn your negative credit items into positive credit flow.

Acknowledgements

First, I would like to thank God for making all this possible, for without Him I am nothing, but with Him, I am unstoppable. To my children, Ryan and Ania, I love you both more than you will ever know. You two are the reason I work so hard. To my sisters, Sayeeda and Terri, and my cousin Robyn, thank you for be a listening ear and shoulder from far away to cry on whenever I needed. Uncle Lewis and Ms. Bea, thank you for being there when we needed a place to run to. And to my parents, Eugene and Bobbie Page. Thank you for never giving up on me, for never turning your back on me and for always believing in me at times when I did not even believe in myself. To all my friends and family, thank you for your support.

About the Author

Janea Adrian Page was born and raised in Gary, IN. A 1992 graduate of Lee Wallace High School, she is the mother of 2 children, Ryan, a freshman in college, and Ania, a fifth grader. She relocated to Indianapolis, IN after living in Nashville, TN for 15 years. When not working, she spends her free time organizing her support group, One Step Forward, finishing up her Bachelor's Degree in Business Management and being an advocate against Domestic Violence.

A Grown Person

A grown person showing anger and persistence to get you back once you have broken it off isn't proof of love, it's a knee jerk reaction. A person trying to kiss your behind and making flaccid attempts to be nicer for 2 weeks or even a month isn't proof they are trying, its proof they know how to diffuse you long enough to hook up once again. Take away a toy, and just like that grown men or women begin to cry. Take away a relationship of convenience and the person who has wronged you begins to whine and cry. Just because they cry, doesn't mean you give them what they want. A lot of men and women don't know what it is like to be loved by a real man or woman. A grown person knows lust, love, passion, and the fear of abandonment. Stop chasing the idea of what love should be and recognize what love is. Love isn't promising to act right after the other person messes up. Love each other right from the start so neither of you will mess up. Love isn't telling a grown person they need to change. Love is a grown person changing on their own because they can't imagine life without each other.

Some men and women sabotage relationships by becoming distant, unreliable, liars and cheaters because they are afraid to make a commitment. Grown people don't play games, they don't have time. Grown people do not string you along like a puppet. You'll know a true gentleman or lady because you will not have to guess, there will be no anxiety, and no competition. Period, Point, blank if the person you are with only wants to love you or be with you because they feel threatened, they are not the person for you.

It is time to CUT-THE-CORD to the man or woman that doesn't mean you any good. Stop believing what he or she says and pay attention to what they do. If that man or woman wanted you, ladies that man would treat you like the queen you are and men, that woman would treat you like the kings you are. They would not want to lose your love, because they value it and treasure you.

www.ingramcontent.com/pod-product-compliance
Lightning Source LLC
Chambersburg PA
CBHW071715040426
42446CB00011B/2077